Instruments in Print

Books from the Whipple Collection

Silvia De Renzi

Whipple Museum of the History of Science

Per mia madre, la Marghi

Published in the United Kingdom by the
Whipple Museum of the History of Science,
Free School Lane, Cambridge.

ISBN 0-906271-16-9

Published to accompany the exhibition of the same name held in the
Whipple Museum of the History of Science,
which opened on 6th November 2000.

Cover Illustration: The Ayscough's Universal Microscope. From *Universal Magazine of Knowledge and Pleasure* 12 (1753).
Reproduced by permission of the Syndics of Cambridge University Library.
Printed by University Printing Services, University Press, Cambridge.

Contents

Acknowledgements

My warmest thanks to Joanna Ball, Sonia Hollins, Clare Jordan and Samantha Weston-Smith of the Whipple Library for their cheerful and constant help, including innumerable trips to the store. Joanna Ball has also very kindly improved my English. Catriona West and all the staff of the Whipple Museum have kindly put up with my many intrusions into the museum's store and given me access to instruments and prints. Cataloguing of the collection was made possible by funding from HEFCE, for which Sarah Newton prepared the application. Many thanks also to Rebecca and Nico Bertoloni Meli. Tamara Hug and David Allington have been patient and helpful with my sudden worries, especially about computers. Dale Johnston and Tim Zielinski has given me invaluable help in transforming a printed catalogue into an exhibition.

For biographical information on Robert Whipple, I am very grateful to Mrs. Elizabeth Whipple, Prof. Rupert Hall and Mary Boas Hall. I thank Mr. John Sprague of Henry Sotheran Limited for kindly providing me with biographical material about Heinrich Zeitlinger.

I have benefited from discussing parts of this catalogue and the final essay with Kemal de Soysa, Aileen Fyfe, Roger Gaskell, Lauren Kassell, Neal Kenny, Elisabeth Leedham-Green, Anna-Katherina Mayer, David McKitterick, Ilaria Meliconi, Adam Mosley, Eugenia Roldán-Vera, Simon Schaffer, Liba Taub, Jon Topham, Andrew Warwick and Francis Willmoth. I am especially indebted to Nick Jardine and Jim Secord for their constant support and numerous suggestions at every stage of the project. I have learnt a great deal from Jim Bennett and Stephen Johnston of the Museum of the History of Science in Oxford. Serafina Cuomo has been a continual source of ideas. Marina Frasca Spada has been amazingly generous and helpful, as always. Nick Hopwood has helped me think about what this catalogue is for, and his countless suggestions have transformed a shapeless draft into a readable book. Responsibility for the mistakes is all mine.

All the images in the text are reproduced courtesy of the Whipple Library. Special thanks to John Bashford and Ian Bolton of the Anatomy Department Audio Visual Media Group for photography, and to Andrew Harvey of University Printing Services.

I thank Robin Myers, Michael Harris and the Oak Knoll Press for permission to use material from my chapter 'Between the Market and the Academy: Robert S. Whipple (1871–1953) as a Collector of Science Books', in *Medicine, Mortality and the Book Trade*, edited by R. Myers and M. Harris, 87–108 (Folkestone: St. Paul Bibliographies, 1998).

Introduction

Instruments in print presents a selection of sixty books from the collection of rare books on scientific instruments which Robert Whipple bequeathed to the University of Cambridge in 1944 to become part of the 'nucleus of a History of Science Museum in Cambridge'. They are now held in the Whipple Library in the Department of History and Philosophy of Science. For a long time these books have been overshadowed by the extensively researched and much appreciated instruments which Whipple presented on the same occasion. Recently, the more than 1400 books have been fully catalogued and electronic records added to the Union Catalogue of Cambridge University Library. They can now be retrieved by typing 'Whipple, Robert Stewart' in the name option. In cataloguing the books, names of printers, publishers and illustrators as well as of former owners have been recorded and made searchable; other copy-specific elements have also been highlighted and subject headings added.

While the on-line records make it possible to gain an overview of the collection and give details of all books, the printed catalogue is intended as a miniature of it. Published in connection with an exhibition held in the Whipple Museum, its main aim is to illustrate how these books can be used as a resource for research at the intersection of book history and the history of science. This is a very focused collection and the wide chronological range of the books—1500 to 1950—allows us to explore changes in the production and use of books on instruments over several centuries. The first three sections of the catalogue investigate some of these changes. The fourth section and the final essay discuss Whipple's collecting project within the history of book collecting, in particular in relation to the emergence of science books as collectable objects. What follows briefly explains how books have been selected and examined.

It is difficult to establish when the expression 'scientific instrument' was first used, but in all probability not before the second half of the nineteenth century (Warner 1990). Before that time instruments were grouped according to their use; there were instruments to draw, to measure or to weigh. In the early modern period instruments were used by professors of astronomy to teach and to observe the sky; and by craftsmen and early professionals such as surveyors or sailors in their everyday activities. But most of the instruments were also objects of entertainment, for example the wealthy would buy and collect clocks and globes for the ingenuity they showed. Philosophical instruments with which to manipulate nature in order to achieve knowledge and control over it, such as the air-pump, started to be produced only in the seventeenth century. Even after the emergence of experimental science, instruments tended to have a life of their own, circulating beyond the cabinets of philosophers and later outside laboratories, and crossing boundaries between what was perceived as the pursuit of knowledge on the one hand and the sphere of entertainment or social prestige on the other (Hankins and Silverman 1995; Turner, A. 1995). It was not before the nineteenth century, when science became largely professionalised and instruments were increasingly used to quantify and not to show, that a more clear-cut divide between scientific instruments and other tools appeared. And yet some instruments, like microscopes, were still produced in many formats and qualities precisely to meet the needs of people with different training and various purposes.

Given the range of meanings and uses which instruments enjoyed in the past, the variety of books on instruments comes as no surprise. Printed material dealing with instruments includes a broad spectrum of kinds of publications and genres of writing, from university textbooks to pamphlets, from handbooks and trade literature for craftsmen to beautifully illustrated volumes to be shown in libraries, from collections of rational recreations to instrument makers' advertisements or sale-catalogues. If one intends to explore this variety, Whipple's collection is probably one of the best resources to use. Whipple did amass an outstanding collection of books by Robert Boyle, and like fellow collectors such as Bern Dibner, was certainly interested in the 'landmarks' of science. But his passion for instruments led him to collect books with a broader mind than the majority of his contemporaries. For example, over the years Whipple also acquired the almost complete book production of Benjamin Martin, an eighteenth-century instrument maker whose public lectures in natural philosophy academic historians of science have only recently investigated. Anything connected with instruments was relevant for Whipple and it was not only because of its moderate price that he would favour a booklet describing a slide rule to a first edition or a beautifully bound volume.

The wealth and specificity of the collection allow one to subvert the hierarchy which has traditionally underlain the presentation of scientific books to the general public. In *Instruments in print* books have not been selected for their descriptions of important and innovative instruments. On the contrary, one of the aims was to give visibility to books dealing with popular and widespread instruments belonging to everyday practice, and to books presenting instruments to a broad audience more than to specialised readers. The former were often rather cheap and perishable; the latter could be more luxurious items, but both appear seldom in catalogues of prestigious collections of science books, which tend to be built according to the canon of the landmarks of science. A successful way of breaking with the canon is to explore books in connection with the history of certain instruments, as in Jim Bennett and Stephen Johnston's *Geometry of war* (1996). The centre of their catalogue, though, is instruments, while the main focus of *Instruments in print* is books. To illustrate the variety of publications dealing with instruments, it was necessary to place next to each other books belonging to different genres, with different formats and aiming at different audiences. Choosing to present neglected books has not, however, led me completely to disregard better known works, though the focus has been on under-researched aspects of their production and editorial history. For example, Tycho Brahe's book on his astronomical instruments is presented here in its second and cheaper edition and receives the same space and attention as an almost forgotten booklet on the carpenters' rule.

Having followed these criteria to select the books, the way in which they have been explored owes much to recent investigations in book history. Influential work in the history of science has focused on the materiality of science. Looking at how instruments and models have been used in relation to experimental knowledge, scholars have stressed that many important rules and guidelines regarding their manipulations are usually transmitted informally, by word of mouth. Such essential knowledge tends to leave no traces. Instruments and models then become the best sources for understanding scientific practice; by reworking what people did with them we can start recapturing the minute adjustments and negotiations necessary to produce knowledge (Sibum 1995).

To publish a catalogue completely focused on books may in the first instance appear a step back. But the aim of *Instruments in print* is not to re-establish any primacy of written texts over practice and objects. Rather, in the same way in which we now understand instruments in the context of their production and use, so we need to make sense of books. To do so we have to change our attitude to books as sources.

Since the first decades of the twentieth century, bibliographers have analysed books as objects and not just as neutral vehicles of ideas. Now that research in book history has become mainstream, books are increasingly studied in relation to the practices surrounding them, including writing, printing, engraving, binding, selling and reading (Hirsch 1967; Chartier 1987; Darnton 1991; Johns 1998). In this framework, publications on instruments fall into a special category, because the acts of making and reading them usually, but not always, implied the presence of other objects, the instruments which they described, taught and discussed. How books on instruments were produced and read and by whom is closely linked to how instruments were produced and used. The first two sections of the catalogue attempt to investigate how these activities have changed.

The first section, 'Making books', highlights issues surrounding the authorship of books on instruments and aspects of their economy: for example, how in the early modern period books on instruments and instruments themselves were often produced and sold by the same people; how the changing relations between natural philosophers and instrument makers affected the relation of both to print; and how the transformation in the sciences in the second half of the nineteenth century led to new institutions issuing publications on instruments. The second section, 'Reading books', is divided into three subsections according to three different types of activities which were carried out with these books. Some were meant to help a wide range of craftsmen, professionals and other practitioners. In others the pedagogical aim is obvious; others again addressed a general audience to whom they offered recreation as well as knowledge.

The third and shorter section on 'Marketing instruments' presents eight examples of printed material produced to advertise instruments. It includes items ranging from the seventeenth to the twentieth century. Of course the economy of instrument making changed dramatically in this period, but in whatever arena and circumstances instruments were used, they had to be sold and bought. The selection aims to show the function of print in connecting learning and commerce. This is also a tribute to Whipple. While much of his private life revolved around antique instruments and rare books, his entire professional life was devoted to boosting profits at the Cambridge Scientific Instrument Company.

To offer a chronologically balanced range of publications in these three sections has been difficult: books up to 1800 are overall more numerous than later ones. To deal with the former I could benefit from the abundant studies carried out at the intersection of book history and history of science for the period up to 1800. Although research on nineteenth- and twentieth-century scientific publications is growing exponentially, fewer works of synthesis are available.

Previous thematic catalogues of books belonging to the Whipple Library include *Sphaera mundi* on astronomical books before 1600 (Bennett and Bertoloni Meli 1994) and *The grounde of artes* on early-modern mathematical books (Johnston, Willmoth and Bennett 1985). Both were published in conjunction with exhibitions held in the Whipple Museum, and included books which had been acquired after Whipple's donation, or even loaned to the Museum for the exhibition. *Instruments in print* is the first catalogue to concentrate exclusively on books presented by Whipple. Collecting books on instruments was a project Whipple pursued with great passion and regarded as complementary to his collection of antique instruments. In this he was not alone; historians are increasingly aware of the importance which so far neglected book and instrument collectors and dealers had in the history of the history of science. As a contribution towards reconstructing their networks, section four of the catalogue presents some of the books which Whipple bought to develop his skills as a collector and to make himself familiar with research in the history of science and specifically of scientific instruments. They comprise a heterogeneous range of twentieth-century publications, such as bibliographies, catalogues of private or public collections, histories of science as well as sale-catalogues of book dealers. To explore further issues related to collecting science relics in the first half of the last century, the concluding essay focuses on Whipple's relations with a circle of dealers and fellow collectors between the 1920s and the 1950s.

Most entries present just one book, but occasionally two or even three books are put together. Titles have generally been transcribed fully. Sixteenth- and seventeenth-century spelling and punctuation have been modernised: 'j' into 'i' and 'u' into 'v'. Abbreviations have been expanded. A minimum of bibliographical information is given for each book. Addresses of publishers and printers have been omitted. The citations which complete the entries refer to the bibliography at the end of the volume.

1

Making Books

Over the centuries instruments have given rise to a wide range of publications, of which the authors have been similarly diverse, from academics to instrument makers, craftsmen to professionals and teachers. Often these books were the result of co-operation between various people, for example a maker and a scholar, even if this was not always fully acknowledged. Given their usually abundant illustrations, which, cut and pasted, could even be turned into pieces of instruments themselves, the work of draughtsmen and engravers was more central than in other books. All this means that exploring the 'authorship' of these books, that is, issues related to how intellectual ownership and credentials were established, can be complex. These matters are obviously connected with broader questions about the changing role of instrument making in natural investigations, and the fluid relationship between makers and scholars or scientists.

Within these frameworks, I have focused on more specific issues, such as the access of instrument makers to print and the role of print in establishing priority over instruments. The former is an important, and under-explored, aspect of the history of instrument makers. For example, to make sense of what they published and where can throw light on their status both in the early modern period, when social boundaries were strict but natural investigations were not the remit of professional scientists, and in times of substantial transformation such as the second half of the nineteenth century. We can explore this also by looking at how makers chose to represent themselves in the books they published, and this is why preference has been given to books including their portraits. Clashes over priority in the design and manufacture of instruments—the other focus of my analysis—have been common since the early modern period. Rooted in the growing commercial value of instruments, these conflicts were also over control of technological knowledge (Long 1991a). While historians have recently started to investigate the early history of patents, the connection between these and the model provided by printing privileges has still to be explored (Long 1991b; Popplow 1998). Over the centuries, instrument makers and scholars worried about making their work public. While a publication could strengthen claims to intellectual and commercial ownership and advertise an instrument, it might also weaken control over its production.

This section also explores how books on instruments were produced and circulated. What is distinctive about them is that they belonged to the economies of both instruments and books. Close links between making instruments and printing books date back to the early sixteenth century, when printers developing their new technology would share skills and competence in metalwork with a heterogeneous community of instrument makers. Such links were reinforced as globes and cheap paper instruments, both based on printed engravings, started to be produced and marketed (Turner, A. 1989; Bryden 1997b). This overlap of expertise and business reached its peak in seventeenth-century London. Instrument makers would usually also produce and sell books on instruments, while their premises, part bookshops, part workshops, became major centres of knowledge. Relations between instrument makers and booksellers were still strong in the eighteenth century, as the co-operation between Benjamin Martin and the booksellers who financed his publications shows. In the nineteenth century, with the increasing industrialisation of book production and the guilds' loss of control over the manufacture of instruments, these connections faded away (Bennett 1985, 1997b; Feather 1988). The last books of the section just gesture towards major questions such as the expansion of periodicals; the links between national and international research institutions, and new genres of technical literature; the role of specialised publishers; and the emergence of collective authorship in scientific works.

1. Johannes Regiomontanus (1436–1476)

Scripta clarissimi mathematici M. Ioannis Regiomontani, de torqueto, astrolabio armillari, regula magna ptolemaica, baculoque astronomico, & observationibus cometarum, aucta necessariis, Ioannis Schoneri Carolostadii additionibus. Item. Observationes motuum solis, ac stellarum tam fixarum, quam erraticarum. Item. Libellus M. Georgii Purbachii de quadrato geometrico.

Norimbergae, apud Ioannem Montanum & Ulricum Neuber, 1544
4°; a-s4 s-y4 1 unsigned leaf

The production of this book takes us straight into the community of astronomers, printers and instrument makers flourishing in the German city of Nuremberg in the sixteenth century. Their activities overlapped in many ways: instrument makers and printers perceived their crafts as cognate because they were both based on metalwork; astronomers regarded the material production of books and instruments as part of their domain.

This is a composite and highly illustrated volume which comprises records of the celestial observations of the astronomer Regiomontanus, his description of astronomical instruments, and the observations of two other important Renaissance astronomers, Georg Peurbach and Bernhard Walther. More than sixty years after Regiomontanus' death, the volume was edited by Johannes Schöner, who also added his own remarks.

Regiomontanus based his astronomical investigations as much on observations of the sky as on accurate printing of previous astronomical treatises. After moving in 1471 to Nuremberg, a city he valued greatly for its instrument makers and printers, he installed a printing press in his own house and embarked on an ambitious publishing project. He was the first person ever to specialise in printing astronomical and mathematical works, and in his shop he also

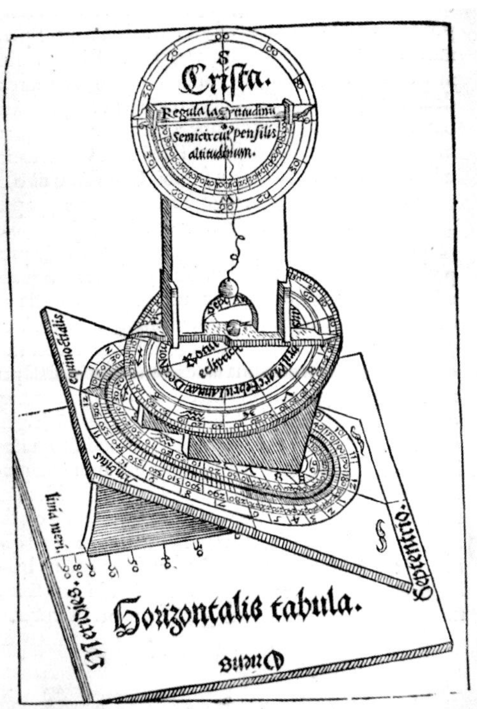

Woodcut of a torquetum, an instrument which represents the different reference planes and circles of the celestial and terrestrial spheres, in Regiomontanus' book.
Catalogue no. 1.

sold instruments. In the Renaissance, such a combination of learned activities, instrument making and printing was not unusual. Schöner, for example, was the author of several mathematical books and at the same time ran a printing shop in the German city of Bamberg, where he made his own type and carved wood blocks for illustrations. In addition to books he 'published' globes, that is, he printed the triangular segments to be mounted on the wooden structure. In 1526 Schöner also moved to Nuremberg, where he taught mathematics and edited several unpublished works of astronomers, including this volume. To produce it, he approached Johann vom Berg (d. 1563) and Ulrich Neuber (d. 1571), two very active printers, whose varied output included theological works, mathematical and astronomical volumes and a catalogue of prodigies. Their co-operation with Schöner must have been very strong: after his death they printed a collection of his mathematical works edited by his son.

Rosen (1981a; 1981b); Eisenstein (1983); Turner, A. (1987; 1989); Gouk (1988); Van der Krogt (1993); Lowood and Rider (1994); Bennett and Bertoloni Meli (1994).

2. Levinus Hulsius (d. 1606)

Tractatus primus [-tertius] instrumentorum mechanicorum Levini Hulsii.

Francofurti ad Moenum, ex officina typogr. Wolfgangi Richteri, impensis autoris, 1605
4°; A-Q4 R2 A4 B6 A-D4

This book includes three treatises on popular early modern mathematical and surveying instruments, such as an inductorium to draw maps, a proportional compass, and a quadrant for measuring altitudes and distances, including of gunshot. They were part of a planned work of fifteen treatises on mechanical instruments, as details of the whole project at the beginning of this volume show; the author's death prevented him from completing it.

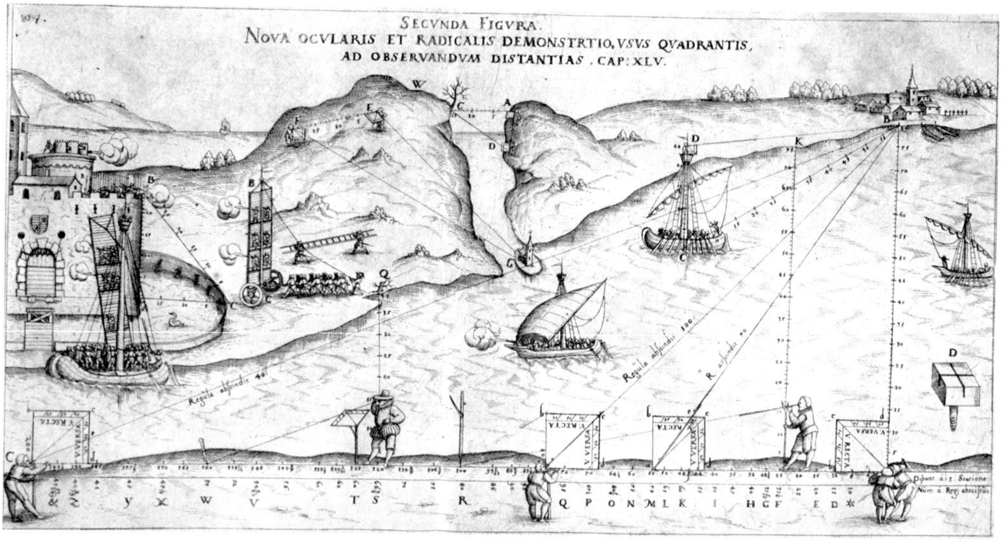

Use of the quadrant in war in Levinus Hulsius' treatise.
Catalogue no. 2.

Born in Ghent, Hulsius was one of Galileo's students in Padua before starting a varied career. He was a teacher of French and compiled a number of dictionaries, wrote geographical atlases and a volume on numismatics, translated and edited a large collection of travellers' reports, and published books on instruments. After working in Nuremberg, he moved in 1602 to Frankfurt, the site of the most important early modern book fair. Here he ran a successful shop where he sold both books and instruments, which he may also have made, though the advertisement at the end of the first treatise in this volume leaves this unclear: 'whoever is interested in the above mentioned instruments can find them at my shop in Frankfurt'. To publish his works, he resorted to the services of a number of printers, some of whom specialised in mathematical and astronomical books; William Richter, for example, who printed this book at Hulsius' expense, also produced Kepler's *De stella nova* in 1606.

To reach a wide audience, Hulsius usually published German and Latin versions of his works. He was proud of making knowledge public, even if, in the case of instruments, this was controversial. In this volume he admitted that he had not invented anything new, and fully acknowledged that the proportional compass described in the third part was an invention of Joost Bürgi, the famous watchmaker of the Emperor Rudolph II. He also included a very detailed bibliography of useful works on the instruments, with names of authors, dates and places of publication. Woodcuts and text engravings were alternated to illustrate the various parts of the instruments and their uses, for example in war. Following a popular practice, readers were also given instructions on how to cut out a large folded engraving representing the back of a *planimetrum* and paste it on a wooden base to make their own instrument.

Poggendorff (1863); Dreyer (1963); Galilei (1978); Van der Krogt (1993).

3. Tycho Brahe (1546–1601)

Tychonis Brahe astronomiæ instauratæ mechanica.

Noribergae, apud Levinum Hulsium, 1602
2°;)::(4 A-E6 F4 G-H6 I4

One of the most interesting transactions which Levinus Hulsius made in his capacity as a bookseller was the purchase of a stock of copies of *Epistolarum astronomicarum libri* (1596) by the Danish astronomer Tycho Brahe, and of the woodcuts and copperplates used for Brahe's *Astronomiae instauratae mechanica.* This work included descriptions of the astronomical instruments with which Brahe equipped his observatory on the island of Hven, with instructions on their construction and use. The book had first been printed near Hamburg in 1598 by Philip von Ohr with the press which Tycho himself had bought for his castle-observatory and taken with him to Germany when he left the island. Early modern astronomers often took a personal interest in printing. However, publishing astronomical and mathematical books was not a simple affair. Even though Brahe had a press of his own, most of his works remained unpublished until his death, while his *Astronomiae instauratae* had been printed in just a few copies. Lavishly bound and decorated with hand-coloured plates, these were presented to potential patrons and colleagues.

Scholars have emphasised that Brahe belonged to the world of courts more than to that of printers and booksellers; he regarded his books as gifts for prospective patrons rather than as commodities. But the fact that an experienced bookseller like Hulsius decided to invest money in giving a 'second life' to the *Astronomiae instauratae* is evidence that a market in books on astronomical instruments existed and that it was booming. In this second edition the quality of the paper was poor, margins were narrow in order to cut costs and Brahe's portrait replacing the smaller emblem on the original title-page could not make up for the fact that this was an altogether different

Brass celestial globe in Tycho Brahe's *Astronomiae instauratae mechanica.*
Catalogue no. 3.

publication. But now, even though the illustrations still made the volume quite expensive, it had become a book to buy. The deal which Hulsius struck with Brahe's heirs was instrumental in enlarging the audience of Brahe's work beyond the few princes and patrons whom the Dane had regarded as his readers.

Dreyer (1963); Thoren (1990); Lowood and Rider (1994); Johns (1998).

4. Leonard Digges (ca 1520–ca 1559)

A geometrical practise, named pantometria, divided into three bookes, longimetra, planimetra and stereometria, containing rules manifolde for mensuration of all lines, superficies and solides: with sundry straunge conclusions both by instrument and without, and also by perspective glasses, to set forth the true description or exact plat of an whole region: framed by Leonard Digges gentleman, lately finished by Thomas Digges his sonne. Who hathe also thereunto adioyned a mathematicall treatise of the five regulare platonicall bodies, and their metamorphosis or transformation into five other equilater uniforme solides geometricall, of his owne invention, hitherto not mentioned of by any geometricians.

Imprinted at London by Henrie Bynneman, 1571
4°; +2 A-Z4 2A-2H4 2I2

At the beginning of the sixteenth century the production of instruments was not as developed in England as it was on the Continent. But by the mid-century the varied world of mathematical practitioners was rapidly coming alive. It included not only noblemen who considered mathematics a suitable topic for their education, and teachers who catered to them, but also skilled artisans, such as surveyors and builders who would use instruments in their activities. Conflicts arose, for example, when mathematically trained practition-

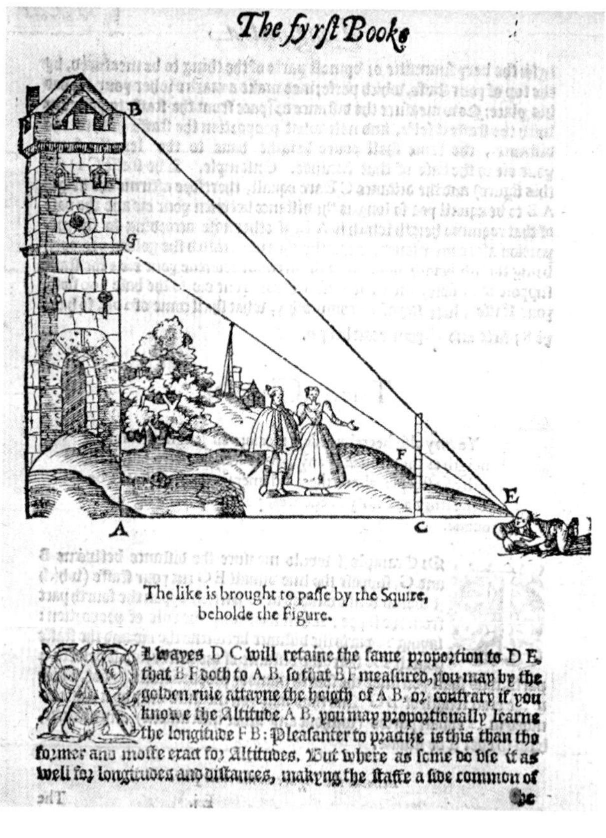

Various typographical fonts in a neat page from Digges' *Pantometria*. Catalogue no. 4.

ers tried to impose instruments on less educated artisans. Whilst instructions on newly designed instruments might remain unpublished to maintain firm control over them, printers slowly started to regard books on instruments as a potentially profitable market. The identity and practice of these printers is an important aspect of the varied world of early modern practical mathematics.

During his life Leonard Digges published a number of works on practical mathematics, but he also left unpublished various manuscripts which his son Thomas (ca 1546–1595) edited after his death. The *Pantometria* was a textbook on surveying, which focused particularly on the use of instruments and on explaining basic mathematical procedures. For the printing Thomas turned to Henry Bynneman, a very active printer, who in 1571 produced thirteen books, the *Pantometria* being his only 'scientific' title. They were all successful and in 1572 Bynneman could open a shop to complement his printing house. On his death he was one of the most prosperous printers of his time. Although religious works and fiction took the lion's share in Bynneman's inventory of 1583, publications on medicine, agriculture and military science were well represented.

Bynneman was renowned for the quality of his printing, and for the *Pantometria* he spared neither ingenuity nor money. In addition to inserting numerous woodcuts, he planned the page layout carefully. He used initials, head- and tail-pieces and three different fonts: a very condensed gothic for the theoretical sections; italic for the examples and roman for titles and subtitles. The *Pantometria* was as much an outcome of its printer's skill as the work of its author. Bynneman's device, a mermaid surrounded by the biblical motto *Omnia tempus habent* (all things have their own time), is prominent on the verso of the last leaf and is of the same size as the coat of arms of the Digges on the recto.

McKerrow (1910; 1913); Turner, A. (1973); Bennett (1987); Johnston (1991; 1994); Barnard and Bell (1991).

5. Robert Hues (1553–1632)

Tractatus de globis, coelesti et terrestri eorumque usu. Primum conscriptus & editus à Roberto Hues Anglo semelque atque iterum à Iudoco Hondio excusus, & nunc elegantibus iconibus & figuris locupletatus: ac de novo recognitus multisque observationibus oportunè illustratus ac passim auctus operâ ac studio Iohannis Isacii Pontani.

Amstelodami, excudebat Iudocus Hondius, 1617
4°; A-T4 V2

Globes were important tools for early modern navigation as well as geographical and astronomical research: countries such as the Netherlands, which was building a commercial empire around the world, became the main centres of production. Globes were also teaching aids and

The device of Jodocus Hondius, map and globe maker in seventeenth-century Amsterdam.
Catalogue no. 5.

luxurious objects to display in libraries and cabinets. They were usually accompanied by handbooks, often written and published by the globe maker himself.

One of the first English globe makers was Emery Molyneux, whose maps were engraved by Jodocus Hondius, a Dutch émigré working in London. Molyneux probably wrote a book to accompany the globes, but no copy is extant. In 1594, Robert Hues, an Oxford student who devoted his life to navigation, published a treatise on Molyneux's globes which became very popular, with eight Latin editions published between 1611 and 1663, six editions in Dutch before 1623, one in French, and three in English. Although Hues' name continued to be prominent on the title-page of the various editions, with subsequent additions and changes his work became the result of the activities of a wide range of people. It is a striking example of the intertwined roles of engravers, printers, scholars and publishers in sustaining the complex economy of producing and circulating geographical knowledge in the early modern period.

One such individual was Hondius himself, who, after returning to Amsterdam to set up a very successful business producing maps and globes, translated an enlarged version of Hues' book into Dutch. After Hondius' death in 1612, his family stepped in to run the business: as it continued to produce globes, so it kept on publishing Hues' treatise, which it now considered an integral part of its business. The 1617 edition included the learned annotations of the Dutch scholar Johannes Isaacus Pontanus (1571–1639). His additions were printed in a smaller font to distinguish them from Hues' text, but references to the 1593 globes for which the book had originally been written were dropped from the title-page. The vignette and motto of the Hondius firm were prominent in the colophon and an advertisement for their globes was included in the preface.

Competition in the seventeenth-century globe trade was fierce, including to sell copied globes. While reproducing maps was relatively easy, Latin names of constellations and countries were easily misspelled. Reliability was an important feature of globe making, as the device chosen by Hondius as a trade mark shows. It represents a dog with his paw on a globe; the dog was itself a symbol of fidelity, and the word *fideliter* (reliably) appears twice in the device, both on top of it and in the motto surrounding the globe.

Taylor (1954); Waters (1958); Bierens de Haan (1960); Van der Krogt (1993).

6. John Tapp (fl. 1596–1631)

The sea-man's kalender: or, an ephemerides of the sun, moon, and certain of the most notable fixed stars. As also, a table of the longitude and latitude of all the most eminent places of the world, first calculated by John Tap. Since corrected, and enlarged with many additions. Viz. new exact tables of the north-star; new tables of 65 of the principal fixed stars, their time of coming upon the meridian every day; with their right ascension and declination, &c. With a discovery of a way to find the long hidden secret of longitude, by Henry Bond, teacher of the mathematicks in the Bulwark near the Tower. All which are now newly calculated and corrected, and many rules and tables added. By Henry Philippes.

London, printed by W. G. for Benjamin Hurlock, and are to be sold at his shop, 1672
4°; A-Z4

Tables and instruments to calculate a ship's position were essential and complementary tools in early modern navigation. This volume is an example of how almanacs containing practical information for sailors including the use of instruments, tables of sines, tide-tables and specific warnings for entering dangerous ports, became a lucrative genre for booksellers and printers. These publications needed constant revision, and tended to become composites, with layers of new information growing on the old. They were also effective vehicles for advertisement.

The activities of the three authors and the bookseller mentioned on the title-page show how deeply intertwined teaching mathematics, printing and selling mathematical books, and making and trading in instruments were in seventeenth-century London. Specialised bookshops provided one of the main sites for such business. John Tapp was a teacher of mathematics, as well as the author of various volumes and a bookseller. A member of the Stationers' Company, the powerful guild of London booksellers, he specialised in nautical and mathematical publications. His *Sea-man's kalender* was first published in 1602. It was very successful and Tapp regularly published revised editions. After his death in 1631 his books and shop went to George Hurlock, who continued to publish mathematical and navigational books, until his son Benjamin took over the business and dealt mostly with schoolbooks and popular literature. Henry Bond (ca 1600–1678) stepped in as the editor of the

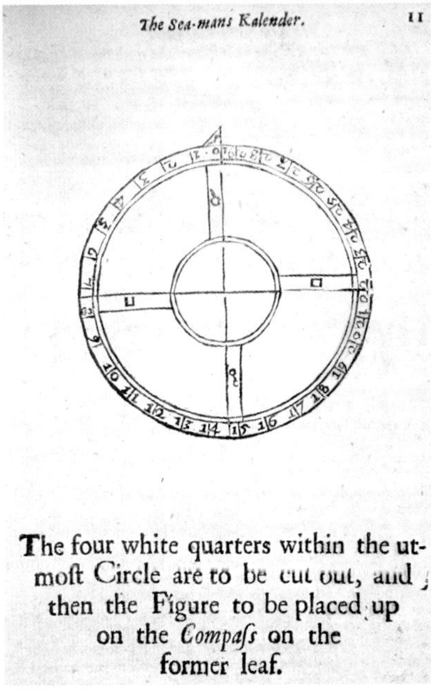
The Sea-mans Kalender. 11

The four white quarters within the utmoſt Circle are to be cut out, and then the Figure to be placed up on the *Compaſs* on the former leaf.

How to turn a page of an almanac into a paper instrument.
Catalogue no. 6.

Kalendar in 1636. Himself a teacher of mathematics, he taught first in the Royal Dockyard at Chatham and then at his house, as the title-page of this book informally advertised. His main contribution to the *Kalendar* was a section on 'the long hidden secret of longitude'. In addition to writing his own books, he edited mathematical works, including in 1653 an enlarged edition of the work of the famous mathematician Edmund Gunter. Henry Philippes (1648–1677), another teacher and prolific writer of mathematical textbooks, took over from Bond as editor of Tapp's book after 1658. In his preface to the 'ingenious sea-man' he stressed that the strong sales of the book had encouraged the publisher in his effort to revise it since its first publication; astronomical tables quickly became out-of-date, but this work showed that it was possible to keep offering reliable information to 'the advantage of the buyer'. For some reason, the name of the globe-maker Thomas Stern, who contributed to this edition revisions of the tables of the longitude and latitude of important places, does not appear on the title-page.

Plomer (1907); Taylor (1954); Waters (1958); Capp (1979); Feingold (1984); Johnston (1991); Willmoth (1993); Adams and Waters (1995).

7. Richard Delamain (fl. 1631)

The making, description, and use of a small portable instrument for ye pocket (or according to any magnitude) in forme of a mixt trapezia thus called a horizontall quadrant. Composed and prodused soly for the benefit and use of such which are studious of mathematicall practice. Written and delivered by Delamain, student and teacher of the mathematickes.

London, printed for Richard Hawkins and are to be sold at his shop, 1632
8°; A4 a4 B-O4

8. William Oughtred (1575–1660)

The description and use of the double horizontall dyall. Whereby not onely the houre of the day is shewn; but also the meridian line is found: and most astronomicall questions, which may be done by the globe are resolved. Invented and written by W. O.

in

Mathematicall recreations. Or, a collection of many problemes, extracted out of the ancient and modern philosophers, as secrets and experiments in arithmetick, geometry, cosmographie, horologiographie, astronomie, navigation, musick, opticks, architecture, statick, mechanicks, chemistry, water-works, fire-works, &c.

London, printed for William Leake, 1653
8°; A8 *8 ¶8 B-T8 U4 X8

9. William Oughtred (1575–1660)

The circles of proportion and the horizontall instrument &c. Both invented, and the uses of both written in latine by W. Oughtred. Translated into English and set forth for the publique benefit by W. F. And now by the authors consent, revised, corrected, and freed from all mistakes in the former edition: and also much amplifyed and explained, by A. H.

Oxford, printed by W. Hall, for R. Davis, 1660
8°; A2 B-R8

These three publications are all about the same instrument, a horizontal dial which made it possible to tell the time and establish the position of the sun without difficult calculations. They are relics of a bitter controversy which was conducted mainly in print between 1631 and 1634. They show that publishing was an indispensable step in claiming priority in the invention of instruments at a time when making them was becoming a substantial commercial enterprise. But the editorial histories of these works stretch beyond the period of the controversy, and are evidence of the role of printers and booksellers in establishing and sustaining customers' interest in instruments.

In 1630, John Haviland printed a book, entitled *Grammelogia*, on the horizontal dial. The author, Richard Delamain, was a teacher of mathematics in London who claimed to have invented the instrument. This prompted a harsh reply from William Forster, one of the pupils of the famous mathematician William Oughtred. Forster quickly edited and published Oughtred's *The circles of proportion*, which included translations into English of the notes on the dial which Oughtred had written when he was building his instrument several years before. Since then the notes had circulated in manuscript, and it was Oughtred's conviction that Delamain had seen both these notes and the instrument at the shop of the maker Elias Allen, where he had been allowed to copy them. While

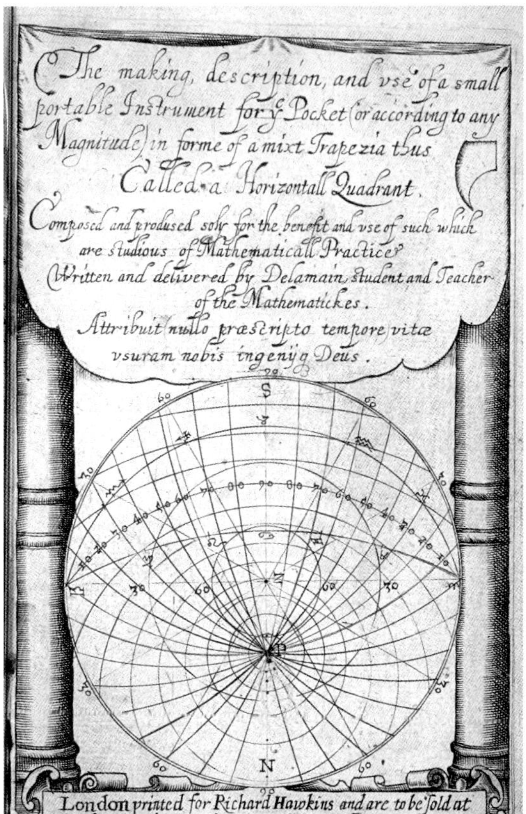

The horizontal dial on the title-page of the book by Richard Delamain, teacher of mathematics. Catalogue no. 7.

Oughtred regarded this as acceptable, he found it outrageous that Delamain claimed priority. In 1632, Delamain published *The making of a small, portable instrument,* in which he retracted the claim. However, a year later, after changing printer, he published a revised edition of his *Grammelogia,* which challenged Oughtred again.

In the meantime, the dial had become a much sought-after instrument; the dispute between Oughtred and Delamain gained it publicity. Publications on the dial came out steadily and in a variety of forms. In 1635 a small pamphlet illustrating its use for the benefit of the by now numerous owners appeared. This was then added to the second edition of the *Mathematicall recreations* published by the bookseller William Leake in 1653. In 1639 Leake had already contributed to keeping the controversy alive by putting on the market a new edition of Delamain's *The making of a small, portable instrument.* In the same year Elias Allen, who was also active in the book trade, financed a new issue of *The circles of proportion,* which was last published in Oxford in 1660. The craze for the instrument started to fade away at the end of the seventeenth century, and in a general survey of mathematical instruments translated and edited by Edmund Stone in 1723 the horizontal instrument was not even mentioned.

Wallis (1968); Bryden (1974); Turner, A. (1981; 1987); Willmoth (1993); Clifton (1995); Hill (1998).

10. Galileo Galilei (1564–1642)

Le operazioni del compasso geometrico et militare. Di Galileo Galilei nobil fiorentino lettor delle matematiche nello studio di Padova.
Terza edizione.

In Padova, per Paolo Frambotto, 1649
4°; *4 A-E8

The well-known controversy following the first edition of this work in 1606 is another example of the complicated links between print and instruments, especially when the priority of their invention and the monopoly over their production were at stake. The mathematical compass which Galilei designed was a mechanical calculator with greater flexibility than any other previous instrument of this kind. In 1599, Galilei had established in his own house a flourishing business in the compasses which the instrument maker Marcantonio Mazzoleni made. Manuscript instructions on the use of the compass were produced by a scribe and circulated, often without Galilei's name. In 1606, he decided that only by publishing a book on the instrument could he secure himself against plagiarism. But he decided to produce the volume in a very small print run, because, as he said, since the book without the instrument would be of no use, only those who bought the instrument would need the book. The sixty copies were printed by the Paduan Pietro Marinelli, who worked at a press located within Galilei's house. Probably out of concern for the monopoly, no illustrations were added.

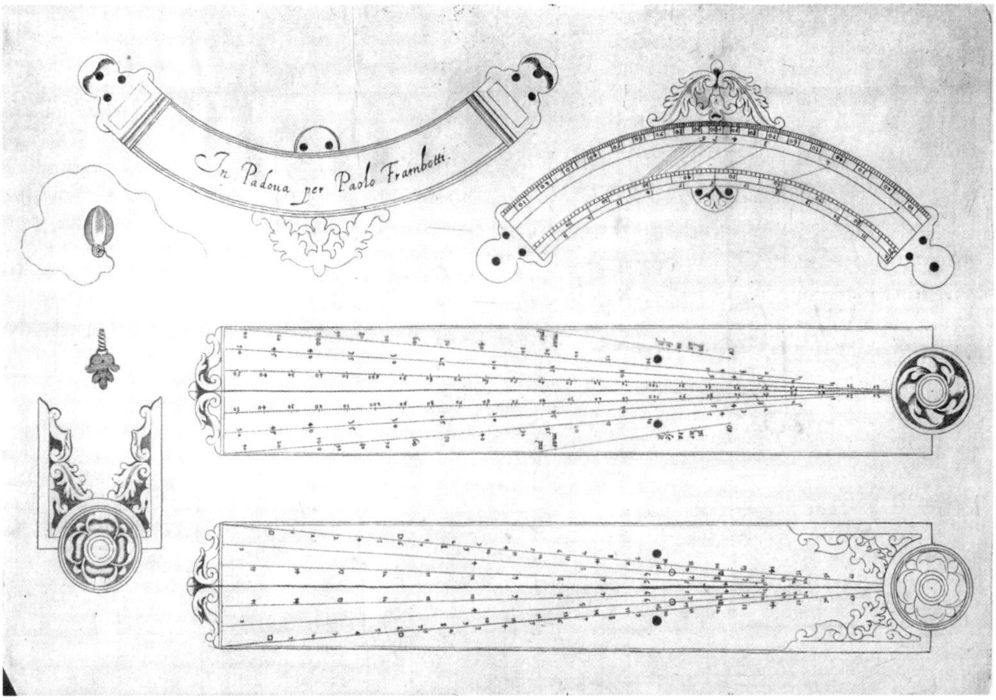

Galilei's compass in the Paduan edition of his work.
Catalogue no. 10.

Soon after the book was out, Baldessar Capra, a former student of Galilei, published in Padua a Latin translation of parts of Galilei's manuscript on the compass and accused Galilei of having stolen the design. But Galilei was able to prove his innocence and Capra was forced to withdraw four hundred of his volumes from the printer's shop. The first accurate illustration of Galilei's compass appeared, however, only in 1613 in a Latin version of Galilei's work by Matthias Bernegger. This was published again in Naples in 1619 and then by Paolo Frambotto in 1640.

A Paduan printer, Frambotto was active in the fields of medicine and science. In publishing Galilei's book he added a dedication to a young and promising patron, Antonio Maria Orsato. A 1649 reprint indicates that the work was in demand even at a time when other books by Galilei were selling quite slowly. From this point of view, the provenance of the copy in the Whipple Library is of great interest: it was owned by a certain Giuseppe Brugnoli, who declared himself to be a student of Pierpaolo Caravaggio (1617–1688). The latter was a military engineer who became a teacher of mathematics and Greek at the *scuole palatine*, one of the most important schools in early modern Milan.

Riccardi (1952); Poggendorff (1863); Galilei (1964–1968); Carli and Favaro (1972); Drake (1978); Galilei (1978); Lowood and Rider (1994); Nummedal and Findlen (2000).

11. William Leybourn (1626–1716)

Panorganon: or, a universal instrument, performing all such conclusions geometrical and astronomical as are usually wrought by the globes, spheres, sectors, quadrants, planispheres, or other the like instruments, yet in being; with ease and exactness. Some uses whereof are exemplified in the solution of such problems as are of frequent use in the practise of geometry, astronomy, dialling, geography, trigonometry, projection, &c. By William Leybourn.

London, printed for William Birch, 1672
4°; 4 unsigned leaves A-S4 T2 2A-2Q4

William Leybourn's bustling activities are another example of the vital links between print, instrument making and mathematical teaching in the entrepreneurial world of late seventeenth-century London. Probably not of wealthy origins, Leybourn became his brother's partner in a prosperous printing house, where they produced several books of mathematics. After leaving this business, Leybourn successfully devoted himself to editing as well as writing mathematical books. He also taught, carried out land surveying, and made instruments. In all these fields competition was fierce, though there is evidence of well-established forms of co-operation between mathematical teachers, instrument makers and booksellers to reach their common audience. For example, since Leybourn did not have a shop of his own, students interested in his course were invited to register at the workshop of the instrument maker Robert Morden.

The *Panorganon* describes a quadrant which Leybourn himself designed, though he acknowledged that he owed much to the manuscript notes of Samuel Foster, professor at Gresham College. A full-page advertisement encouraged readers to buy the quadrant and other instruments in silver, brass or wood from Walter Hayes, one of the most active instrument makers of the time. More than a casual piece of advice from Leybourn, this was probably the result of a deal between Leybourn and Hayes and is evidence of their co-operation. Hayes had started his career as an engraver, and in addition to making and selling instruments, he sold books and funded their publication. He appears in the imprint of another

Portrait of William Leybourn, surveyor and teacher of mathematics in seventeenth-century London. Catalogue no. 11.

volume by Leybourn, and was the publisher of Seth Partridge's *Description and use of an instrument called the double scale of proportion* (1671), and of John Twysden's pamphlet on the use of the planisphere (1685). Although his name is prominent in Leybourn's *Panorganon*, Hayes was not responsible for its publication. For this Leybourn turned to William Birch, a very productive London bookseller, though not specialised in mathematical works.

The self-portraits, revised as he aged, which Leybourn added as frontispieces to most of his books are an obvious sign that he had acquired confidence (his first book had been published under a pseudonym) and another way of advertising his activities.

Kenney (1950); Taylor (1954); Bryden (1992); Willmoth (1993); Lowood and Rider (1994); Clifton (1995); Johns (1998).

12. Johannes Hevelius (1611–1687)

Johannis Hevelii machinae coelestis pars prior; organographiam, sive instrumentorum astronomicorum omnium, quibus auctor hactenus sidera rimatus, ac dimensus est, accuratam delineationem, et descriptionem, plurimis iconibus, aeri incisis, illustratam & exornatam exhibens.

Gedani, auctoris typis, & sumptibus, imprimebat Simon Reiniger, 1673
2°; [A]2 B4 A-Z4 2A-2Z4 3A-3M4

The growing use of the telescope in seventeenth-century astronomy called for a new visual language with which to represent the results of observations as vividly and faithfully as possible. Johannes Hevelius was a Polish astronomer who published some of the most spectacular images of celes-

The hard work of building astronomical instruments, as represented in Hevelius' *Machinae coelestis pars prior.* Catalogue no. 12.

tial bodies and astronomical instruments in the early modern period. He carried out his celestial observations with brass instruments, most of which he designed and constructed himself, though he acknowledged the help of other people, including his second wife, a Dutch printer (possibly the printer of this book, Simon Reiniger), and the Italian Tito Livio Burattino. The latter was an architect working at the court of the Polish king and the creator of various instruments, including lenses and one of the longest telescopes hitherto constructed, which is fully described in the *Machinae coelestis.* Detailed instructions for the construction and use of Hevelius' instruments are here complemented by remarkable engravings, which show them in a variety of settings, both domestic, such as Hevelius' observatory on the top of his house, and more public, for example an urban landscape where a telescope was built.

Hevelius was well aware of the problems and difficulties of transferring what he saw with his telescope first onto paper and then into print, and claimed to supervise every step of this lengthy process. Control over the printing process was as important to Hevelius as it had been to other early modern astronomers, including Regiomontanus (catalogue no. 1) and Tycho Brahe (catalogue no. 3). Hevelius possessed types and a printing press. While he hired a printer, Reiniger, to complete the production of his *Machinae coelestis,* he did not seek the financial help of a bookseller but kept copies in his observatory to be sent to potential readers. Some of them miraculously survived a fire which burnt down the observatory and destroyed many of Hevelius' instruments and papers in 1681. He was also a skilled draughtsman and signed many of the illustrations he published, although we cannot be certain that he engraved them too. It was in the vibrant milieu of Gdansk that Hevelius found the best collaborators for his *Machinae coelestis,* the painter Andreas Steck (1635–1679) and the engraver Isaac Saal (fl. 1678), who both signed the images. Steck was famous for his portraits of the Polish nobility; together with Saal he also produced the illustrations of one of the most important Polish botanical books, Jacob Breyn's *Exoticarum aliarumque ... plantarum* (Gdansk, 1678).

Barocas, Ingegno, Caccamo (1972); Grzybkowska (1979); Hook and Norman (1991); Winkler and van Helden (1993); Johns (1998); Monaco (1998).

13. Nicolas Bion (ca 1652–1733)

Traité de la construction et des principaux usages des instrumens de mathématique. Avec les figures nécessaires pour l'intelligence de ce traité. Dedié au Roy. Quatriéme édition, revûe, corrigée & augmentée par le S.r N. Bion.

A Paris, chez Charles-Antoine Jombert et Nion Fils, 1752
4°; [A]4 A-Z4 2A-2Z4 3A-3L4 3M2

This is the fourth edition of a very successful work on mathematical instruments first published in 1709. During the eighteenth century it ran to several French editions, was

Portrait of Nicolas Bion, instrument maker in eighteenth-century Paris, engraved by Nicolas Larmessin, engraver to the King. Catalogue no. 13.

pirated by a Dutch publisher and translated into English and German. Its author was an instrument maker active in Paris at a time when the production of instruments, both everyday devices such as drawing instruments, and precision instruments including lenses and barometers, was flourishing. Collaboration between natural philosophers and makers was also intense. We do not know much about Nicolas Bion, except that he was appointed 'Engineer to the King', ran a much-frequented workshop and died a rich man, leaving a well-established business to his son. Unlike many of his colleagues and competitors, Bion wrote extensively about the instruments he made. In addition to this comprehensive treatise, which included a fairly complete list of the mathematical instruments available at the time, he published works on globes and astrolabes. Ultimately, Bion was as famous for his books as for his instruments.

After Bion's death his son published a new edition of the treatise; he revised the final chapter and added a flattering portrait of his father, engraved by none other than Nicolas Larmessin, one of the most prosperous engravers in Paris who also worked for the King. Bion's son was concerned that to cut expenses, plates had been crammed with images. In a rather apologetic manner he explained that the plates could still convey a clear sense of the objects represented; they could also be pulled out of the book to make it easy for readers to follow the text and look at the images at the same time.

That this was a successful work is clear from the bookseller who chose to invest in its fourth edition, Charles Antoine Jombert (1712–1784), who belonged to the Parisian bookselling elite. His house was the centre of a circle of scholars, artists and bibliophiles, and he was renowned for the quality of his printing. His press produced a large number of mathematical and technical books.

Daumas (1972); Payen (1981); Augarde (1989); Bassy (1990); Turner, A. (1998).

14. Jesse Ramsden (1735–1800)

Description of an engine for dividing mathematical instruments. By Mr. J. Ramsden, mathematical instrument-maker. Published by order of the commissioners of longitude.

London, printed by William Richardson; and sold by John Nourse and Mess. Mount and Page, 1777
4°; 2 unsigned leaves A-B4

As the demand for scientific instruments grew in eighteenth-century England, the status of instrument makers diversified. Those who catered for a broad audience of gentlemen interested in natural philosophy often had a remarkable commercial success, but never won the full respect of scholars; those who provided mathematicians and astronomers with increasingly accurate instruments built equal relations with them and could even be admitted to the Royal Society. These two classes of instrument maker also developed different relations with print. For example, while the bibliography of Benjamin Martin, a member of the first category (catalogue no. 30), includes more than sixty tracts, pamphlets and books, which he wrote as part of his broader commercial enterprise, Jesse Ramsden, who represents the second category, published only just over a dozen works, including new editions and translations.

After working as a clerk in a warehouse, Ramsden apprenticed himself to a mathematical instrument maker and then opened a shop in Piccadilly. He became a very innovative maker of navigational instruments. His main achievement was the design and construction of a machine tool which mechanised the process of marking off angles on quadrants and sextants; it changed the production of instruments forever. In 1786 he was elected a Fellow of the Royal Society and later even of the Imperial Academy of St. Petersburg. He never worried much about publishing his work. Sometimes publications came as part of the broader recognition which he enjoyed from powerful patrons. For example, in the case of the engine which gave him fame, the Board of Longitude rewarded him with £615. It also ordered that five hundred copies of the description, explanation and drawing of the engine be published to reach a wider audience. The firm of Mount and Page, which held a sort of monopoly in books on navigation in eighteenth-century England and traditionally worked for state bodies, financed the publication of the slim, but richly illustrated, pamphlet. They would sell it

Jesse Ramsden's engine: the first step towards mechanisation in the manufacture of instruments.
Catalogue no. 14.

for five shillings. The same combination of state patronage and commercial interest from Mount and Page is to be found again in the publication of Ramsden's book on the engine for dividing straight lines on mathematical instruments, published in 1779. On other occasions, it was only thanks to particularly satisfied customers that descriptions of Ramsden's instruments became public.

This apparent lack of interest in the power of print developed along with Ramsden's awareness of the risks connected to publishing details of one's inventions. His neat pamphlet on the engine has remarkably large engravings of both the engine and its parts; these were made after Ramsden's own drawings and the text is rich in minute explanations. But it is missing a critical piece of information about the construction of the engine.

Taylor (1966); Webster (1981); Bennett (1985); Turner, A. (1987); Chapman (1990; 1993); Adams (1993); Sorrenson (1995); Clifton (1995).

15. Cornelius Varley (1781–1873)

Graphic telescope. From the Transactions of the Society of Arts, Manufactures, Commerce, &c. Vol. L.

London, printed by J. Moyes, 1834
20 p.

To achieve its main aim, the Society for the Encouragement of Arts, Manufactures and Commerce, which was founded in London in 1783, would award an annual prize to the best contribution to the arts, science and industry. Inventions of new instruments, particularly of optical instruments, were especially appreciated. Increasingly, making innovations public became the society's main aim, quite apart from the prizes. By the 1820s the Society's *Transactions* regularly called for papers on instruments. In nineteenth-century England, encouraging instrument makers to publish their work was very unusual. The numerous new scientific societies, including the Geological Society and even the British Association for the Advancement of Science, tended to have strict rules of admission, excluding makers and mechanics. Some of them nevertheless contributed articles to the growing scientific periodical literature, but their status in the community of scientists generally declined; this process was possibly slower in microscopy.

In 1811 Cornelius Varley had received a patent for his graphic telescope, which allowed a draughtsman to see an enlarged object through the telescope and at the same time the paper onto which it could be drawn. Although Varley had already published on the instrument, in 1834 he was invited to submit a new account, including a plate of the telescope and its parts, to the *Transactions* of the Society, of which he was a member. His twenty-page paper also circulated as a separate offprint.

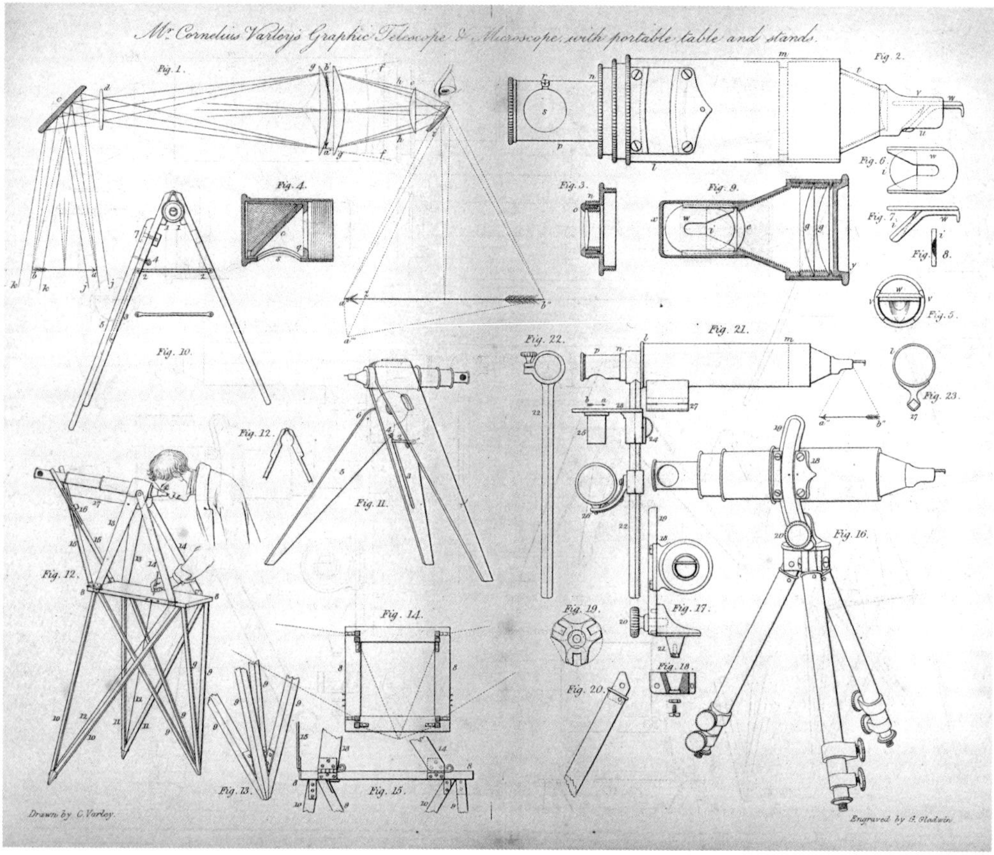

Cornelius Varley's drawing of his own graphic telescope and microscope.
Catalogue no. 15.

Varley represents the elite of instrument makers: he came from a family of instrument makers and was also a renowned watercolourist. In his workshop in north London he produced first optical instruments and the machinery for their manufacture, and later also electrical instruments. He worked on meteorology and electricity. A founding member of the Royal Microscopical Society in 1839, he also published extensively in the *Journal of the Royal Microscopical Society*. He probably owned a remarkable collection of books: three of them are in the Whipple Library: Benjamin Martin's *Philosophia britannica*, which Varley bought in 1820; Willem Jacob 's Gravesande's *Mathematical elements of natural philosophy confirm'd by experiments*, bought in 1819; and a presentation copy of Henry Lawson's *Observations on the placing of thermometers*, published in 1845. The Whipple Library also owns a manuscript by Varley on dialling.

DNB; Hudson and Luckhurst (1954); Bennet (1985; 1989); Brock (1989); Turner, G. L'E. (1989a); Clifton (1995); Varley Jeffery (1997).

16. William Ford Stanley (1829–1909)

Surveying and levelling instruments theoretically and practically described for construction, qualities, selection, preservation, adjustments, and uses; with other apparatus and appliances used by civil engineers and surveyors. By William Ford Stanley.

London, E. & F. N. Spon. And of the author, 1890
xi, 552 p.

Stanley was a nineteenth-century instrument maker who achieved both wealth and status. A member of the Physical Society of London, the Geological Society and the Royal Astronomical Society, he complemented his business activities with research and publications. He patented the application of aluminium to the manufacture of instruments and was recognised as an authority on making surveying instruments, the stability of which he greatly improved. During his life he cultivated various pastimes, including painting, astronomy and phrenology, and he left his money to found a technical school.

Surveying and levelling is a hybrid publication. It is not simply a sale-catalogue because it provides descriptions of instruments other than those Stanley made, though it does include a price list of his items. It is also much more detailed than a regular sale-catalogue, although nineteenth-century sale-catalogues tended to become substantial publications, often sturdily bound in fancy covers. Neither is it a handbook on instruments for professional surveyors, because, as Stanley acknowledged, he lacked the experience and authority to deal with this topic. The main audience of the book, which was successful and ran to various editions, was the community of instrument makers who wanted to keep abreast of innovations. Stanley provided them with descriptions of state-of-the-art instruments and of recent improvements to them. But he admitted that he could deal only with major changes and 'typical instruments': he could not discuss the finer adjustments which makers would

SKETCHING APPARATUS. 443

pattern shown in Fig. 266 is that of Captain W. Verner, made by Messrs. Elliott Bros., to whom the author is indebted for the loan of the engraving. It consists of a small board $9\frac{1}{4}$ inches by $7\frac{1}{2}$ inches, at two sides of which there are small rollers to hold paper 7 inches wide and from 3 feet to 6 feet in length, according to its thickness.

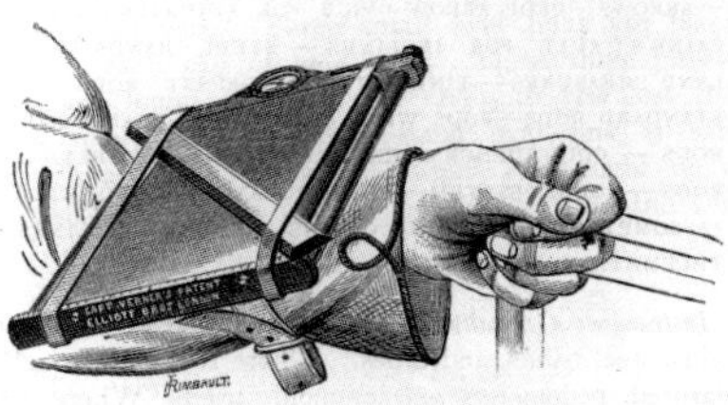

Fig. 266.—*Cavalry sketching case.*

Two stout India-rubber bands are passed over the board, which hold a small straight-edge to scale to any position on the paper with sufficient firmness to be able to draw a line against it. A small compass on one side of the board indicates direction. After one sketch is made, a new part of the paper is rolled forward.

609.—**Camera Lucida—Optical Compass.**—In new countries where land-marks are not clear a sketch of the general aspect of the country will make the points of triangulation more clear. Where the plane table is not used these sketches may be made with accuracy as to positions by the use of the camera lucida, or points of observation may be taken in correct bearing by the optical compasses. These instruments are described in the author's "Treatise on Drawing Instruments," sixth edition, pages 142-7.

A sketching case to be used on a horseback, marketed by William Stanley. Catalogue no. 16.

carry out at the request of their customers. The manufacture of instruments maintained an artisanal quality even when their standardisation was advanced. Stanley also included suggestions about how to organise the labour in a workshop, with details of the tools required and general remarks on how to finish, polish, engrave and pack the instruments.

References to the damage which tropical temperatures could inflict remind us that surveying instruments were typically sent to the colonies to carry out mapping and other surveying activities which were central to the colonial administration. It was in connection with these new and often large-scale operations that the demand for surveying instruments increased in the nineteenth century and their quality and accuracy were greatly improved. Stanley was able to meet this growing demand: his products were displayed at the Great Exhibition in 1851.

DNB; Inwards (1911); Allen (1953); Bennett and Brown (1982); Hackmann (1985); McConnell (1985).

17. Charles Edouard Guillaume (1861–1938)

Traité pratique de la thermométrie de précision, par Ch.-Ed. Guillaume.

Paris, Gauthier-Villars et Fils, 1889
xv, 336 p.

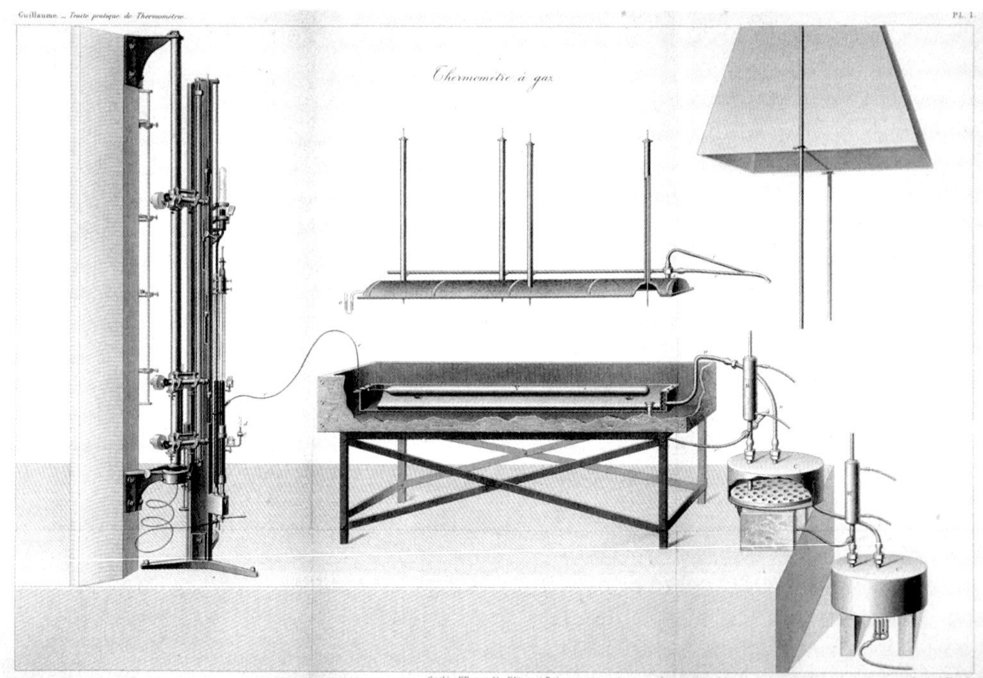

An instrument in an abstract space: a gas thermometer in Charles Guillaume's handbook. Catalogue no. 17.

18. Department of Commerce

Technologic Papers of the Bureau of Standards. No. 170. Pyrometric practice. By Paul D. Foote, C. O. Fairchild and T. R. Harrison.

Washington, Government Printing Office, 1921
326 p.

A fundamental feature of nineteenth-century physics was physicists' increasing concern with the reliability and precision of their instruments, and the transformation of apparatus into objects of theoretical study in their own right. This trend was linked to the growing interest in the standardisation of measurements in science and industry; it was also one of the causes of substantial changes in the organisation of instrument manufacture and in the relations between instrument makers and scientists. New national and international bodies devoted to settling controversies which could arise in the standardisation process were founded; they often issued a whole range of publications, including periodicals, handbooks and manuals.

In 1875 the Bureau International des Poids et Mesures was established on the outskirts of Paris. It was run by an international committee with the aim of establishing basic standards

An instrument in a factory: controlling the temperature with a six-point indicator.
Catalogue no. 18.

and determining, in co-operation with national laboratories, fundamental physical constants. These national laboratories, including the Physical Laboratory in Britain, the German Imperial Physical-Technical Institute and the American National Bureau of Standards, offered services to national industries. After 1881 the results of research at the Bureau International were published in its *Travaux et mémoires.* In the first issue a very interesting distinction between papers for which the international committee would take responsibility and papers published by individual researchers was drawn. The first were to be read and approved by the whole committee through a rather complicated procedure. In the event of clashes within the committee, a ballot would be cast. Both the *Travaux et mémoires* and a number of other publications documenting the activities of the Bureau were published by Gauthier-Villars et Fils, one of the two French publishers holding a virtual monopoly on publications in mathematics, physics and chemistry.

Thermometry was a particularly important topic because a number of other standards depended on accurately-known temperature. The basis of this handbook by the Swiss physicist Charles Edouard Guillaume was work he had done at the Bureau, of which he became director in 1905. He specialised in metallurgy and in 1920 received a Nobel Prize. At a time when science was mostly published in periodicals, hardback books tended to be marketed as presenting authoritative and definitive views on certain topics.

The American Bureau of Standards was founded in 1901; after World War I, and especially under the direction of Samuel Stratton, the relations of the Bureau with the Department of Commerce grew steadily. The Bureau would flood industries and laboratories with publications. All produced by the Government Printing Office, some were periodicals, such as the *Technologic papers* and later the monthly *Journal of research.* They were intended to give guidelines on the use and calibration of instruments and machinery. Initially they appeared as slim separate publications, in paper covers with the pages just stapled together; later on they were also offered in cloth-bound volumes. Official publications of the Bureau also included monographs and handbooks on the one hand, and newsletters comprising shorter reports on work in progress on the other.

Paul (1980); Pyatt (1983); Lecoq (1991); Tesnière (1993); Dörries (1994); Bailey (1995).

2

Reading Books

How were books on instruments read in the past? One thing is certain, they were not always meant to be read in the presence of the instruments they were about. What happened when books, which are much more mobile artefacts than instruments, substituted for them? Historians have recently recognised that reading is a historically and culturally embedded practice; it changes over time and according to different purposes (Grafton and Jardine 1990; Darnton 1991; Manguel 1996; Raven, Small, Tadmor 1996). We can think of how books were read in the past in terms of groups of readers, for example students, craftsmen, professionals and women. But matching ready-made categories of readers with books ignores the fact that whatever their intended audiences, books usually end up in the 'wrong' hands. So we cannot deduce from what authors wrote in their prefaces who were their actual readers. Addressing certain audiences could be part of authors' strategies to promote themselves or to add value to their books rather than a faithful depiction of the audience the book would actually reach. The rhetoric of prefaces and introductions must be decoded and combined with material features of books, such as their language, quality of paper and of illustrations, and format. These elements are clues to the books' price and their circulation.

Another way of exploring how books were read is to focus on the broader sets of activities, such as learning or taking action, into which reading was incorporated. This section focuses on three major activities to be carried out while reading books on instruments: 'doing things', learning, and amusing oneself. The advantage of grouping books according to the practices they were supposed to accompany is that we can appreciate how active reading is and the variety of purposes it implies. Unfortunately, traces of provenance or marginalia are too scarce in these twenty-three books to allow us to investigate actual readers.

Books for 'doing things'

A substantial number of books on instruments were meant to be used by artisans, professionals and other practitioners, as they carried out their tasks. These publications would not necessarily present innovations, but provided clear instructions, practical examples and helpful tables or other aids related to the use of common tools. Some of them were written by artisans themselves; although much of craftsmen's training was spoken and has left no traces, these often successful publications are examples of trade literature. In other books, the authors' attempt to impose a 'proper' practice onto lower status practitioners is evident. Together these kinds of books represent bodies of practical knowledge built around instruments and circulating in print.

19. Jacob Köbel (ca 1465–1533)

Astrolabii declaratio, eiusdemque usus mire iucundus, non modo astrologis, medicis, geographis, cæterisque literarum cultoribus multum utilis ac necessarius: verum etiam mechanicis quibusdam opificibus non parum commodus: à Iacobo Koebelio facilioribus formulis nuper aucta longeque evidentior aedita.

Moguntiae, Petrus Iordan excudebat, Mense Iulii 1535
4°; A-G4

In 1513, Johannes Stöffler, a German professor of mathematics, wrote a book on the astrolabe. Among the steady flow of publications catering for the needs of the wide range of Renaissance practitioners, including navigators and surveyors, who used this versatile instrument, Stöffler's book became a classic. It was printed by Jacob Köbel, a town clerk in the city of Oppenheim, who also worked as a surveyor and printer. He himself wrote a number of mathematical books, among which this treatise on the astrolabe.

Köbel's preface argued that his book did not contain anything original or new, but was meant to provide beginners with an easy and clear presentation of the instrument.

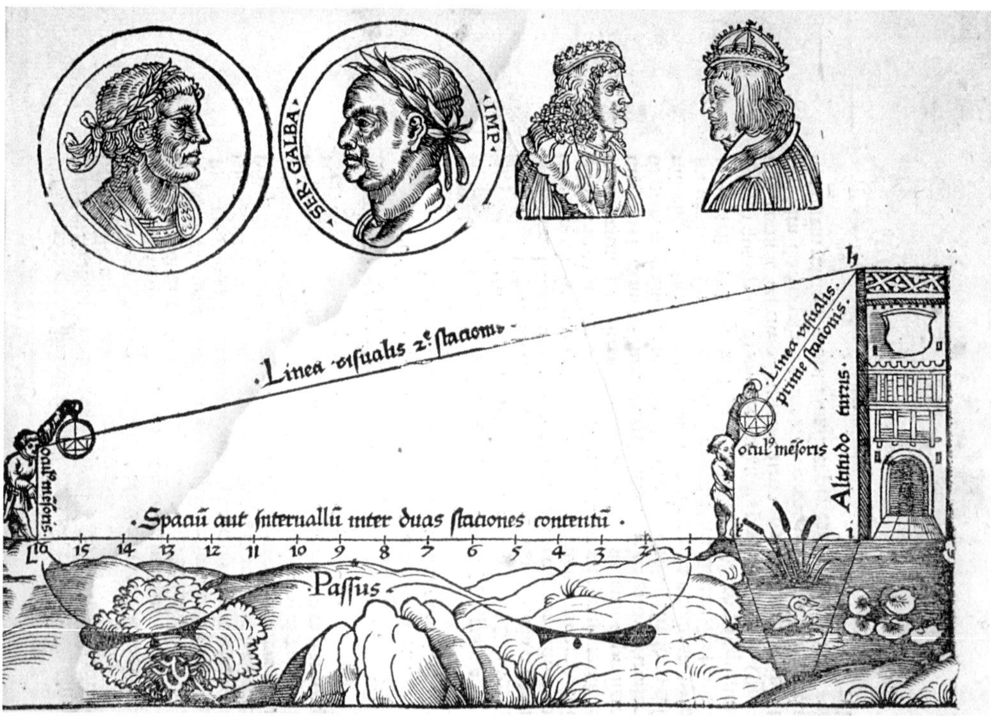

Figurines of Roman Emperors and Renaissance dignitaries filling up
Köbel's woodcut on the use of the astrolabe.
Catalogue no. 19.

According to the title, knowledge of the astrolabe was useful and necessary not just to astronomers, physicians and geographers, but also to men of learning and to craftsmen. This latter category would probably include master-builders, miners and artisans, though it is difficult to judge to what extent these people could read Latin. None of the eight pre-1600 editions of Köbel's *Astrolabii declaratio* was in German. The astrolabe enjoyed a higher status than other instruments and Köbel's immediate audience was probably made up of those mathematical practitioners, instrument makers, and surveyors, who, like himself, had strong links with academia and a sound knowledge of Latin. By 'astrologers', Köbel meant both astronomers and astrologers, and it is worth noting that according to the title of the first edition, the book included a section on judicial astrology; but Köbel never added this. The reference to an audience of physicians reflects the role which astrology had in medieval and Renaissance medical practice. Although generally doctors would not calculate the position of the stars themselves but relied on star tables, a Latin book on the astrolabe would fit well into a physician's library.

The 1535 edition of Köbel's text was posthumous, and was expanded, possibly by the printer Peter Jordanus, with pictures and sections taken directly from Stöffler's volume. Jordanus had been a partner of Köbel, and inherited some of his printing tools. The decoration of the book was enriched with a wide range of figurines, including images of Roman emperors and animals, which do not obviously relate to the astrolabe. It would be worth exploring to which section of the book's intended audience this modification would most have appealed.

Zinner (1941); Benzing (1962); Gunther (1932); Vogel (1981); Bennett and Bertoloni Meli (1994); Simcock (1994); Kusukawa (2000).

20. Bartolomeo Crescenzi, detto Romano (ca 1565–?)

Proteo militare di Bartolomeo Romano diviso in tre libri. Nel primo si descrive la fabrica di detto Proteo, & in esso nuovo istrumento, tutti gli altri istrumenti, di matematica che imaginar si possano. Nel secondo, e terzo si tratta dell'uso di detto istrumento, nel quale si formano tutte le figure di geometria, & gl'istrumenti di prospettiva, pittura, scoltura, e d'architettura. S'insegna ancora l'arte del navigare, e quella del guerreggiare con nuovo, e facilissimo modo, come più distintamente nella tavola si potrà vedere.

In Napoli, appresso Gio. Iacomo Carlino & Antonio Pace, 1595
4°; ¶4 2¶4 A-Z4 Aa4

Proteus was a sea-god who often changed his form and the title of this volume, 'Military Proteus' refers to the versatility of the instrument it describes. Made of different parts, it could be transformed into various mathematical instruments, including an armillary

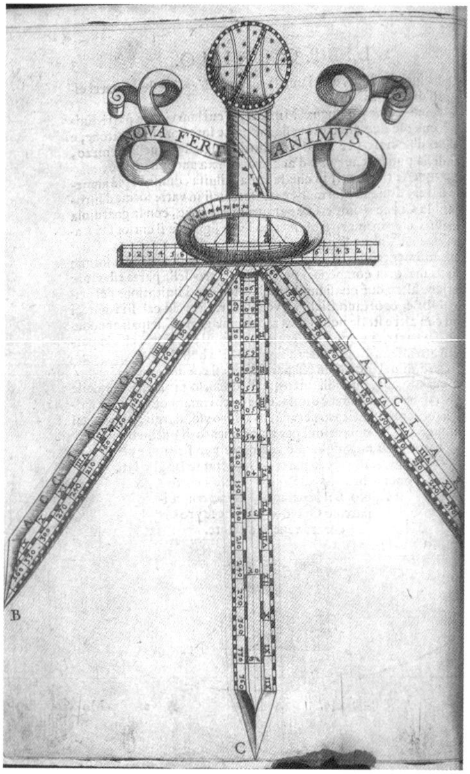

An instrument for seventeenth-century gentlemen: the multifunctional dagger of Bartolomeo Romano. Catalogue no. 20.

sphere, and used in a range of fields as varied as architecture, navigation and warfare. It embodied the mathematization which had taken place in most practical activities during the sixteenth century. But it also satisfied contemporaries' fascination for ingenuity and surprising contrasts: in this case the multiplicity of uses of the object and its relatively small size. Bartolomeo Romano was also well aware that an instrument which strongly resembled a dagger could appeal to an audience of noblemen for whom it was a symbol of status and wealth. In describing the construction of the instrument, Bartolomeo suggested that a prince could have it partly covered in gold, while those who would really use it as a mathematical instrument could make do with another metal or a sturdy wood.

Throughout his life Bartolomeo enjoyed papal patronage: he was employed as an officer of the papal navy before specialising in engineering. In co-operation with architects, he was particularly active in the construction of a harbour and in the regulation of rivers. At the end of the sixteenth century, the Papal State expanded and underwent major reorganisation. Noblemen and clerics were increasingly assigned technical tasks, and both patronage and competence were key elements in carving out a career. The *Proteo militare* was dedicated to Emilio Pucci, the admiral of the papal navy. In the same way in which Bartolomeo thought of his instrument as both an elegant object and a useful tool, he addressed his book to a double audience: while pleasing noblemen readers, he also instructed a community of fellow mathematical practitioners. As he wrote, the clever engineer, the knowledgeable architect, the cunning captain and the wary pilot could all find the instrument useful.

Bartolomeo was committed to promoting mathematical knowledge at various levels: while his other published work on navigation was intended for fellow naval captains, he also wrote a didactic treatise on mathematics for ordinary seamen, though it was never published.

Guglielmotti (1882); Polverini Fosi (1984); Bennett and Bertoloni Meli (1994); Bennett and Johnston (1996).

21. John Brown (fl. 1648–1695)

The description and use of the carpenters-rule: together with the use of the line of numbers (inscribed thereon) in arithmatick and geometry. And the application thereof to the measuring of superficies and solids, gaging of vessels, military orders, interest and annuities: with tables of reduction, &c. To which is added, the use of a (portable) geometrical sun-dial, with a nocturnal on the backside, for the exact and ready finding the hour of the day and night: and other mathematical conclusions. Also of a universal dial for the use of seamen or others, with the use of sliding or glasiers-rule. Collected and fitted to the meanest capacity by J. B.

London, printed by W. G. for William Fisher, 1662
12°; A6 B-K12 L6

The opening remarks of this booklet are, together with its material aspect, evidence of the existence of an early modern audience of artisans with great professional interest in instruments, little education and little money to spend on books. Usually, books in this duodecimo format and with crowded pages were at the cheaper end of the market.

In the second part of the booklet, where the account of a slide rule is attributed to John Brown, the identity of 'J. B.' becomes clear. A well known instrument maker active in London in the second half of the century, John Brown specialised in barometers, quadrants, sectors and sundials. In his appeal to the 'courteous reader, whomsoever thou art', he reports with great vividness a scene which probably occurred several times in his shop. Would-be purchasers would ask him instructions about the use of the Gunter sector he had on sale, and Brown would refer them to Gunter's work. However, because Gunter's book was expensive and the instructions it provided obscure, many of the potential customers were deterred from buying the instrument and concluded that it was superfluous. Brown was therefore urged to remedy this situation by publishing his volume and

Frontispiece of John Brown's booklet showing a carpenter and his tools. Catalogue no. 21.

promoting what he called an 'instrumental way of working', which he intended to be particularly useful to mechanics with little knowledge of arithmetic. These would include joiners, masons and bricklayers. Stock references to these categories of artisans appeared in prefaces and title-pages of books, even when they were not the true intended audience. But this booklet offering a series of very concrete problems and examples could well have become part of the libraries of John Brown's customers.

The first edition came out in 1656, three more editions followed in the seventeenth century, and one more in the eighteenth. Brown was the author of several other handbooks on instruments, most of which were in the same duodecimo format; he would sell them at his shop, the *Sphere and Sun Dial.*

Taylor (1954); Bennett, H.S. (1965; 1970); Hackenberg (1986); Willmoth (1993); Clifton (1995).

22. Adam Martindale (1623–1686)

The country-survey-book: or, land-meters vade-mecum. Wherein the principles and practical rules for surveying of land, are so plainly (though briefly) delivered, that any one of ordinary parts (understanding how to add, subtract, multiply and divide) may by the help of this small treatise alone, and a few cheap instruments easy to be procured, measure a parcel of land, and with judgment and expedition plot it, and give up the content thereof. With an appendix, containing twelve problems touching compound interest and annuities; and a method to contract the work of fellowship and alligation alternate, very considerable in many cases. Illustrated with copper plates. By Adam Martindale.

London, printed for R. Clavel, and T. Sawbridge, 1702
12°; A-O6 P4

In the early modern period the need for land surveying grew and tensions developed between mathematically trained and less educated practitioners. Adam Martindale's book first appeared in 1682 and is an example of the increasing demand for handbooks, including easy publications for young surveyors.

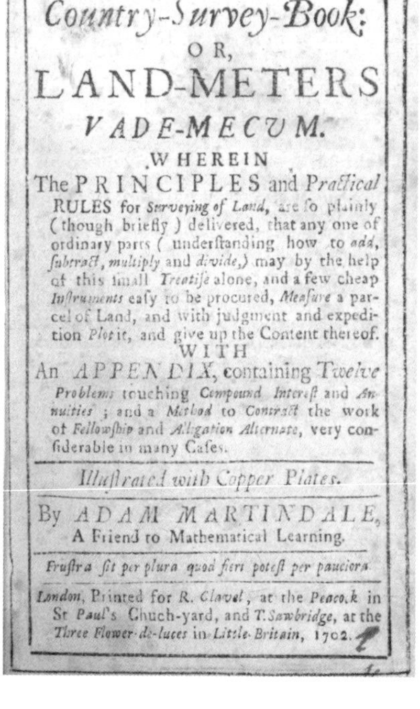
THE
Country-Survey-Book:
OR,
LAND-METERS
VADE-MECUM.
WHEREIN
The PRINCIPLES and Practical RULES for Surveying of Land, are so plainly (though briefly) delivered, that any one of ordinary parts (understanding how to add, subtract, multiply and divide,) may by the help of this small Treatise alone, and a few cheap Instruments easy to be procured, Measure a parcel of Land, and with judgment and expedition Plot it, and give up the Content thereof.
WITH
An APPENDIX, containing Twelve Problems touching Compound Interest and Annuities; and a Method to Contract the work of Fellowship and Alligation Alternate, very considerable in many Cases.
Illustrated with Copper Plates.
By ADAM MARTINDALE,
A Friend to Mathematical Learning.
Frustra fit per plura quod fieri potest per pauciora.
London, Printed for R. Clavel, at the Peacock in St Paul's Chuch-yard, and T. Sawbridge, at the Three Flower-de-luces in Little-Britain, 1702.

How to become a surveyor in eighteenth-century England: the frontispiece of Adam Martindale's 'country-survey-book'.
Catalogue no. 22.

A very popular nonconformist preacher, Martindale earned a living teaching mathematics. The leaf advertising Martindale's lectures was left by mistake in the 1702 edition of his *The country-survey-book* even though he had died sixteen years before. Gentlemen and 'others' (probably students from lower strata) were invited to board at his house and be instructed in various parts of mathematics. These were the main intended audience of this successful volume (the 1711 edition was defined as the eighth).

As Martindale wrote in the preface, various mathematical treatises were available in English, but they contained sophisticated topics which would only confuse beginners. They were also bulky volumes, either in folio or quarto; even those in octavo were too big to be carried around, and their prices would put off impoverished young students. For all these reasons Martindale had taken great care to produce a small format book which many would be able to afford, and to lay out the contents in a gradual way. He had limited himself to basic instructions and the descriptions of simple instruments: his account of the diagonal scale, for example, was, as he said, just a fragment of the description which could be found in William Leybourn's comprehensive treatise on surveying, but one which would help readers understand. A drawback of keeping costs low was that, to Martindale's chagrin, the printer had produced only three plates onto which all the diagrams were crammed.

Before publishing his book, Martindale had asked both Fellows of the Royal Society and experienced surveyors to peruse it. John Collins, an FRS with strong links to the book trade, was invited to add a preface. He wrote that the book was small, cheap and good: it would be useful to students and the vulgar for whom it was intended.

DNB; Taylor (1954); Richeson (1966); Eden (1975–1976); Bennett (1991); Willmoth (1993).

23. John Robertson (1712–1776)

A treatise of such mathematical instruments, as are usually put into a portable case: containing their various uses in arithmetic, geometry, trigonometry, architecture, surveying, &c. &c. Designed for the benefit of engineers, architects, surveyors, and for young students in the mathematics. To which is prefixed, a short account of the authors who have treated on the proportional compasses and sector. By J. Robertson, F.R.S.

London, printed for T. Heath; J. Hodges; and J. Fuller, 1747
8°; A2 A8 B4 B-G8 H4 I2

In eighteenth-century England architects, landscape gardeners, surveyors and engineers proliferated. Country-house building and urban development expanded at an unprecedented rate and increasingly, in addition to the state, private citizens were able to afford the services of these professionals. They had very varied social backgrounds and mathematical

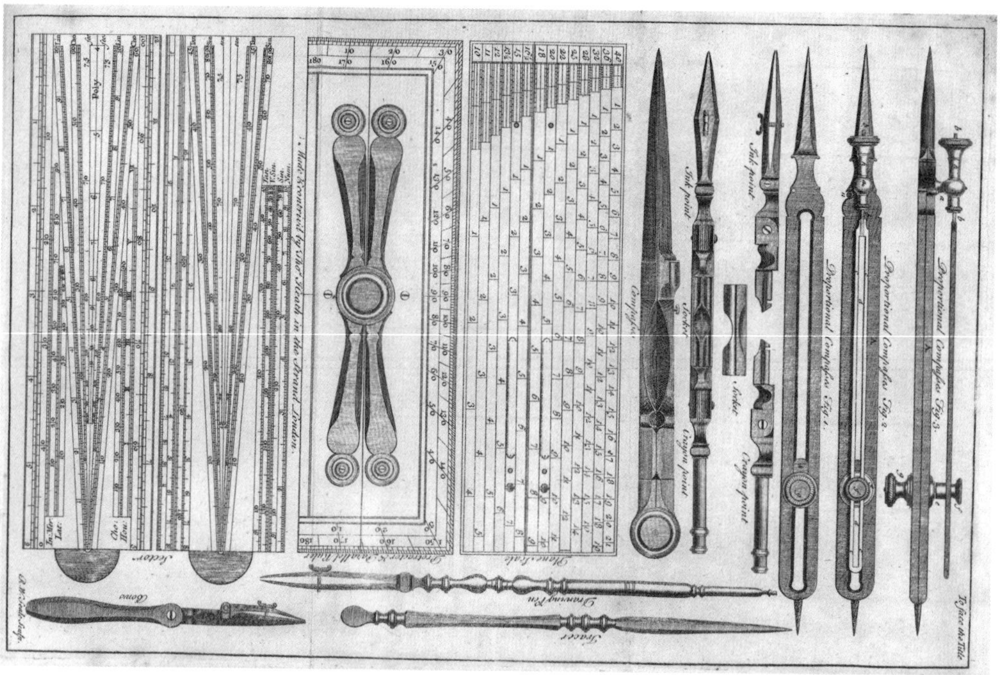

The pull-out frontispiece of Robertson's book on drawing instruments, including an advertisement of the maker Thomas Heath.
Catalogue no. 23.

educations: questions of status arose. Mathematical and drawing instruments were the basic tools of their profession: during the eighteenth century portable cases including sets of the most useful instruments became fashionable. Instrument makers were quick to satisfy architects' and engineers' demands, and diversified their wares. Since most of the instruments were standard and ready-made, the main differences were in their combination in the cases. These could be produced in various sizes and materials. The smallest case would contain a pair of compasses, a drawing pen and a plane scale. The more complete set would include a sector and a protractor too, while the type called 'box-case' was divided into two compartments with special partitions for the instruments.

Booksellers were also quick to grasp the new opportunity for business and started to market books specifically designed to accompany the cases. Often completed with a range of mathematical problems, these publications could be used as teaching aids by schoolmasters or by a wider audience as manuals. John Robertson was master of the Royal Mathematical School at Christ's Hospital in London and then of the Royal Navy Academy; in 1768 he was appointed librarian to the Royal Society. He opened his book with an erudite discussion of the history of most of the instruments, going back to the Renaissance. In combination with the dedication to Martin Folkes, President of the Royal Society, it shows that Robertson wanted to address the upper crust of the profession.

The pull-out frontispiece of this volume shows the instruments contained in a case and is at the same time an advertisement of Thomas Heath, a very active instrument maker. His name appears again at the end of the volume where his skills in executing instruments are praised: it comes as no surprise to find that, together with the booksellers J. Hodges and J. Fuller, he funded the publication of the volume.

DNB; Taylor (1966); Holmes (1982); Crawforth (1985).

24. Thomas Moss (fl. 1765–1776)

The description and use of a new instrument for taking internally the diameters of lying casks, in the middle between the bung and head. Likewise a new and very extensive table, exhibiting the internal lengths of lying casks. By Thomas Moss.

London, printed for the author, and sold at his house. Also by W. Stuart; and J. Johnson, 1776
8°; A-K4 L4 1 unsigned leaf

In the eighteenth century the Excise Office was one of the largest and most professionalised departments of the British government. Patronage was important in the advancement of the employees' careers, but standardised training would allow young men to climb the ladder from the low positions of excise gaugers or revenue collectors to positions of higher rank. How to gauge casks and barrels of irregular shape in order to calculate the tax due was a major problem and a matter of conflicts with merchants. A wide range of publications dealt with this issue, including a work by the famous Newtonian mathematician Colin Maclaurin who, in 1735, produced what was deemed an 'elegant geometrical solution' to the question. And yet forty years later ways of measuring were still controversial. In particular, it seems that learned officers of the Excise tried to impose accurate, that is mathematical and quite complicated, ways of gauging casks on reluctant employees who preferred simpler procedures.

Thomas Moss was the inspector general of imported liquors in Davenport, Kent. In 1766 he published a successful treatise on gauging, probably one of the numerous mathematical handbooks written by excise officers for the mathematical education of their employees. It went through two subsequent editions. Moss was so

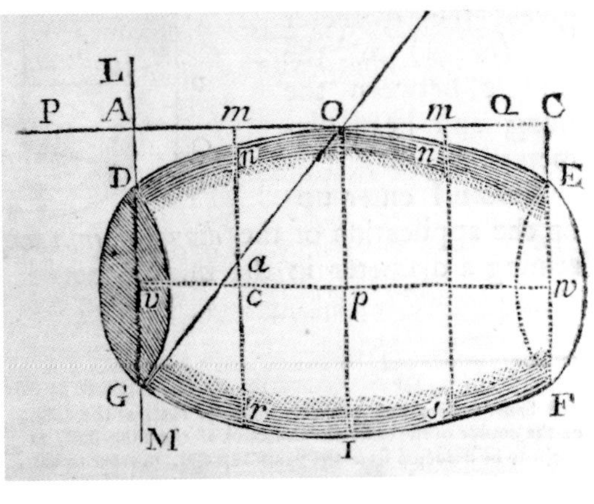

How to measure the contents of a barrel according to Thomas Moss, officer of the Excise. Catalogue no. 24.

concerned about the inaccuracy of current ways of gauging that he also published, partly at his expense, a book on an instrument of his own design which could allegedly improve measuring practice. Moss argued that while gaugers claimed to be able to judge the size of a cask just by viewing it, they were more interested in the speed of the operation than in its accuracy. Guessing and pretending were methods he did not approve of. No reference is made to Maclaurin's book, but Moss claimed that his method was based on the principles of the immortal Newton. Aware of the resistance which many gaugers had already offered to his new instrument, he addressed an audience of 'intelligent, candid and inquisitive', that is of mathematically trained, readers, who would share his enthusiasm for Newtonian principles and back the accuracy of his method.

Moss appended to his preface an advertisement for the book he was planning to publish next, a text on geometry and algebra. He was looking for subscription, a common way of financing books in the eighteenth century, but the project was not successful. Probably the demarcation of mathematical books between intellectual recreations and practical aids such as this did not help Moss reach the genteel audience which would usually finance the publication of books.

Holmes (1982); Brewer (1989); Guicciardini (1989); Wallis and Wallis (1993); Grabiner (1998).

25. *Handbook of artillery instruments. 1914.*

London, printed under the authority of His Majesty's Stationery Office by Harrison and Sons, 1914
8, v, 187, 9–15 p.

This book was written for a special category of practitioners: army officers. It was one of a series of *Military books* which included a wide range of publications covering all aspects of military life and warfare. Handbooks of weapons, reports on health policy in the Army, military and naval dictionaries, regulations and laws of various military institutions, surveying and topographical reports, accounts of field operations and histories of famous battles were published under the authority of the King's Stationery Office for the instruction of officers and soldiers. A list of books in the series is appended at the end of the volume. Some of them dated back to the 1880s, but most underwent regular revision and ran to several editions.

The technology of war changed dramatically at the beginning of the twentieth century. Apart from lethal chemical weapons, one of the major innovations in World War I was a broad range of precision instruments, including binoculars, telescopic sights and range finders. The connections between science and war became stronger than ever. The British Government invested heavily in research on new types of optical glass and struck deals with

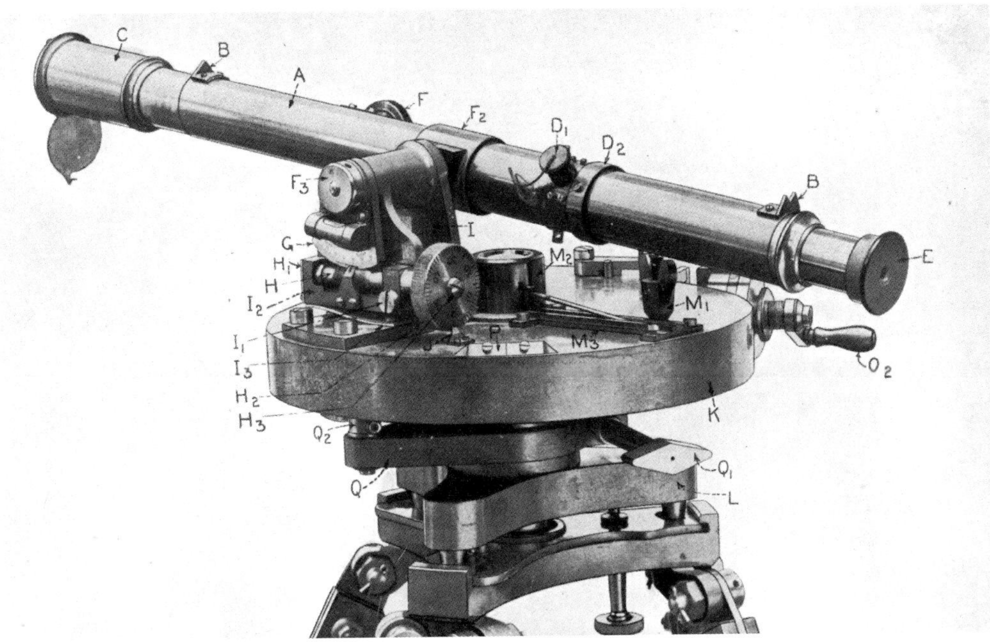

Optical instruments of war: a telescope for observation of fire.
Catalogue no. 25.

scientific instrument companies for the supply of the apparatus it needed. Soldiers had to be taught to use these new instruments, particularly in the evaluation of what they saw through range finders. Instruction was a matter of life and death.

This volume, which was published in April 1914, a few months before the outbreak of war, represents the handbooks which instructors were supposed to use in their training programmes. No theoretical aspect of optics is discussed, but the book provides comprehensive practical information on precision instruments, including how each part functioned, how to mount and dismount them, and how to repair and carry the equipment without damaging it. It also lists a set of tests for range takers using range finders. Readers were referred to other manuals dealing with instruments used by the armed forces, and urged to send additions or suggestions to the Royal Arsenal at Woolwich.

Whipple acquired this book only as a second-hand copy in 1930, but he must have had a special interest in it. He had been professionally involved in the application of optical glass to weapons. German firms had been the major suppliers of high-quality optical glass to Great Britain before 1914 and deals were still being struck in 1915. As the Managing Director of the Cambridge Scientific Instrument Company, Whipple was sent to the United States in 1915 to investigate the possibility of securing supplies, but no satisfactory agreement was concluded.

Terraine (1982); Russell (1989); Williams (1994).

Books for learning

School and university teaching of mathematics, natural philosophy, and later physics and other sciences, has always been based on textbooks. For example, Renaissance textbooks of mathematics would include descriptions of astronomical models and a few other instruments. Even when in the eighteenth century less formal teaching became popular, such as lectures given in coffee-houses or by itinerant teachers, a range of printed material would help the participants memorise what they had seen and heard. However, the ways in which these various students were supposed to integrate the spoken words of their teachers with the printed words and images in books, and with manipulation of instruments, changed with the frameworks of education. It was not before the nineteenth century that students were regularly asked to put their hands on instruments, and this led to the production of new kinds of teaching material, including loose sheets of practical instructions to be used in laboratories.

26. Oronce Fine (1494–1555)

Orontii Finei Delphinatis, regii mathematicarum professoris, de solaribus horologiis, & quadrantibus, libri quatuor.

Parisiis, apud Gulielmum Cavellat [1560]
4°; ã4 e4 a-z4 A-E4

French Renaissance gentlemen and professionals, including physicians and lawyers, would complement their humanistic education with basic mathematics. Oronce Fine held the first chair of mathematics at the Collège de France, which King François I had founded in Paris to provide an alternative to the stale university curriculum. Fine was a renowned instrument maker and at the centre of a community of mathematical practitioners. Shortly after his appointment at the Collège, he published his *Protomathesis*, a big volume in folio including treatises on arithmetic, geometry, cosmography and dialling. It became a successful textbook and the model for later works devoted to teaching mathematics. Each treatise was also published separately and ran to various editions.

Although the audience for textbooks of mathematics was on the increase, booksellers were generally wary of embarking on mathematical books; they often had illustrations and were expensive. Among the more audacious was the Parisian Guillaume Cavellat. On various occasions, including his address to the reader of this volume, he complained about the financial risks of publishing books of mathematics and astronomy; but he developed a successful editorial strategy. He would offset the costs of publishing commentaries to rare and difficult mathematical texts of antiquity by producing run-

The neat illustration of a complicated dial in Oronce Fine's work.
Catalogue no. 26.

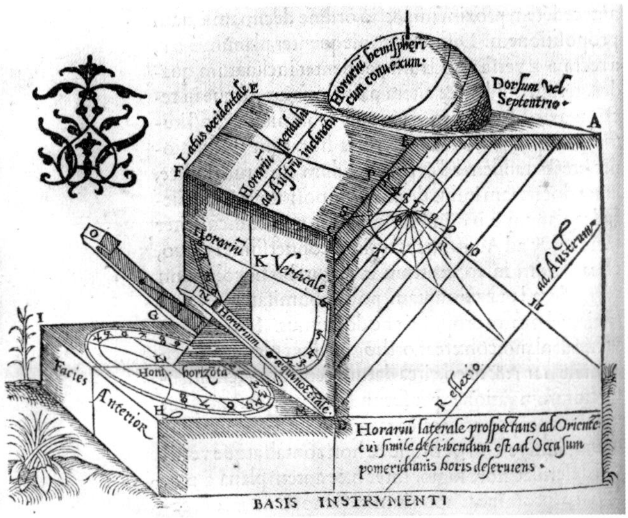

of-the-mill textbooks which secured him a constant flow of cash. Cavellat knew that readers were keen on having freshly published volumes and to meet this demand without going to the trouble of producing new editions, he would print copies of successful books without a date of publication; the copy in the Whipple is one of these. Then immediately before selling the volume, he would add the date.

This is a posthumous edition of *De solaribus horologiis,* the treatise of the *Protomathesis* dealing with the construction and use of sundials and similar instruments to measure the time. This was a much sought-after skill and sundials were popular among both gentlemen, for whom decorated sundials were common gifts, and merchants. Fine wrote in Latin, assuming that his readers would be fluent in this language, but his style was remarkably easy. The layout of Fine's work was also particularly neat: himself an engraver, he ensured that fine illustrations complemented clear instructions to make technical knowledge appeal.

Hillard and Poulle (1971); Margolin (1976); Heninger (1977); Poulle (1981); Gouk (1988); Pantin (1988); Kusukawa (2000).

27. Gaspar Schott (1608–1666)

P. Gasparis Schotti Regiscuriani e Societate Jesu cursus mathematicus, sive absoluta omnium mathematicarum disciplinarum encyclopædia, in libros XXVIII. digesta, eoque ordine disposita, ut quivis, vel mediocri præditus ingenio, totam mathesin à primis fundamentis proprio marte addiscere possit.

Herbipoli, sumptibus hæredum Joannis Godefridi Schönwetteri. Excudebat Jobus Hertz, 1661
2°;)(-2)(6 A-M6 N8 O-3H6 3I4 a-d6 e4

Throughout the early modern period devastating wars between Catholic and Protestant countries raged in Europe. On both sides education was regarded as an effective propaganda weapon. To the Jesuits, who had founded numerous colleges to teach young Catholic noblemen, knowledge was not only the best introduction to the true faith, but also its strongest bastion. Mathematics was an important part of their curriculum.

Gaspar Schott was a disciple of the famous Athanasius Kircher and taught mathematics in various colleges in Italy and Germany. This was the textbook he designed for his students at the Jesuit college of Würzburg. He claimed to have kept the book to a manageable size; to cut costs he had also reduced the number of plates. Yet, it was a bulky volume and more a mathematical encyclopaedia than a handbook. In addition to the traditional mathematical curriculum of arithmetic, geometry, music and astronomy, Schott included chapters on mechanics, warfare, navigation and surveying. The book was intended for beginners: students were encouraged to familiarise themselves with Euclid's elements, but Schott reassured them that if they were not able to tackle Euclid, they could always skip the demonstrations and still be able to follow the course. Those with a keener interest were referred to other works, including Schott's own four-volume *Magia Universalis*. However, each chapter of the book was complemented by explanations of the construction and use of the relevant instruments. An appendix by the Jesuit Adamus Adamandus Kochánski dealt with a machine for perpetual motion, the focus of much research in the early modern period.

Compared to the flamboyant descriptions of machinery in most of Schott's works, this textbook looks sober. For example, the section on optics is short and no reference is made to the trickeries produced by Schott's much-loved optical devices. And yet, together with its cross references and its forty-three plates, the book allows us to make sense of what young Catholic noblemen were expected to learn about instruments. As prospective soldiers in the service of the Counter Reformation, they would be informed about surveying and gunnery techniques; as future devout courtiers, they would learn how to enjoy the wonders of magic, mathematics and natural philosophy.

Casciato, Ianniello, Vitale (1986); Findlen (1994); Hankins and Silverman (1995); O'Malley (1999).

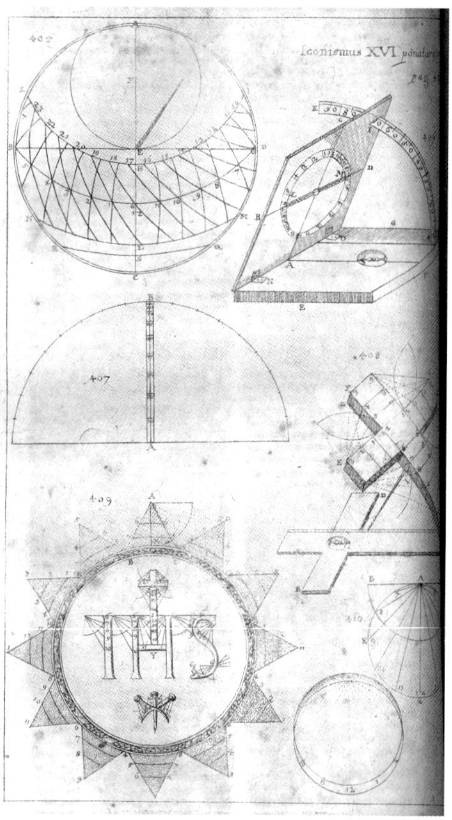

Learning to dial from Gaspar Schott's *Cursus mathematicus*: one of the dials is made of a cross and the letters IHS, an abbreviation of 'In Hoc Sepulcro' (In this grave).
Catalogue no. 27

28. Willem Jacob 's Gravesande (1688–1742)

G. J. 's Gravesande Philosophiae Newtonianae institutiones, in usus academicos. Editio secunda auctior.

Leidae & Amstelodami, apud Joh. Arn. Langerak, Joh. & Herm. Verbeek, & Balthasarem Lakeman, 1728
8°; *8 A-O8 1 unsigned leaf P-Z8 2A-2H8 2I4

Eighteenth-century Dutch universities were among the first in Europe to make Newtonianism the basis of courses of natural philosophy. Experiments became the core of the lectures. Students were not allowed to put their hands on the apparatus, but professors such as Willem Jacob 's Gravesande performed hundreds of experiments before them. To do so he used a broad range of apparatus, which he designed and built.

's Gravesande complemented his experimental research and teaching by publishing extremely popular textbooks. In so doing he reached a wider audience and succeeded in linking his name to the dissemination of the new philosophy. His books were translated into English and French and were used in universities outside the Dutch Republic. In the eighteenth century natural philosophy was becoming increasingly fashionable among broad circles of non-experts; 's Gravesande's books, which did not require much mathematical competence, quickly became sought-after introductions to the discipline outside academia too.

Together with his publishers 's Gravesande knew that the market was varied, and that people with different levels of knowledge might be interested in these publications. What they were offered had to be diversified to create, and respond to, new demands. To this end, size and appearance of the volumes had to be carefully planned. In 1720 's Gravesande published his *Physicae elementa mathematica, experimentis confirmata, sive introductio ad philosophiam Newtonianam,* two bulky volumes in quarto. It was meant to help students remember what they had seen. 's Gravesande published two enlarged editions in 1725 and 1742, now with an audience of scholars in mind. But he was aware that students and beginners needed something different and decided to publish an abridged

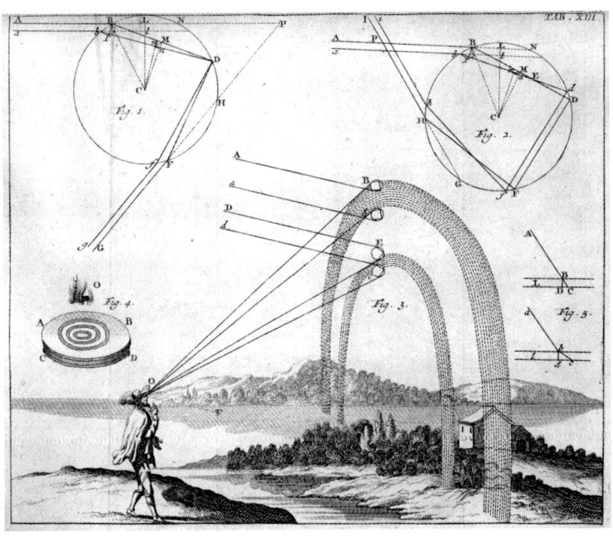

A pull-out plate to explain the law of refraction of colours in 's Gravesande's textbook.
Catalogue no. 28.

version of the work. The *Philosophiae Newtonianae institutiones ad usus academicos* is a thick, but portable book in duodecimo. Even if in the second edition it became a slightly bigger volume in octavo, in his 'to the reader', 's Gravesande recognised that the size of the original *Physicae elementa* was not suited for its use: to satisfy beginners, a small and much more handy volume was sufficient. It included all the important conclusions of the experiments, with references to them in the form of the brief notation, 'exp'. While readers were helped by illustrations and an index, cross references to the more comprehensive version were given for more thorough explanations and the full descriptions of the experiments.

's Gravesande's textbook was used at Cambridge. The owner of this copy was Andrew Pemberton, who entered Peterhouse College in 1749, received his BA in 1753 and MA in 1756, and then became a barrister-at-law. He bought the book in 1750. Possibly to acknowledge 's Gravesande's clarity, he added a note 'bene scripsisti' (you wrote well) to the title-vignette of the volume. The motto in the vignette reads 'varietas delectat' (variety is fun); Pemberton added the words 'at non obscuritas' (and not being obscure).

Wordsworth (1968); Ruestow (1973); Wallis and Wallis (1977); Hall (1981); De Clercq (1997).

29. Francis Hauksbee (1688–1763)

A course of mechanical, magnetical, optical, hydrostatical, and pneumatical experiments. To be perform'd by Francis Hauksbee; and the explanatory lectures read by William Whiston.

[London] [1715?]
4°; [A]2 B-L2

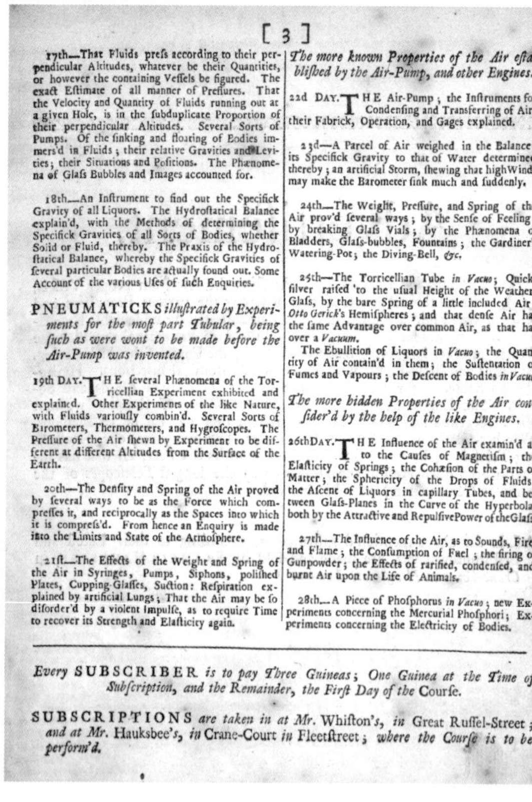

[3]

17th—That Fluids preſs according to their perpendicular Altitudes, whatever be their Quantities, or however the containing Veſſels be figured. The exact Eſtimate of all manner of Preſſures. That the Velocity and Quantity of Fluids running out at a given Hole, is in the ſubduplicate Proportion of their perpendicular Altitudes. Several Sorts of Pumps. Of the ſinking and floating of Bodies immers'd in Fluids; their relative Gravities and Levities; their Situations and Poſitions. The Phænomena of Glaſs Bubbles and Images accounted for.

18th—An Inſtrument to find out the Specifick Gravity of all Liquors. The Hydroſtatical Balance explain'd, with the Methods of determining the Specifick Gravities of all Sorts of Bodies, whether Solid or Fluid, thereby. The Praxis of the Hydroſtatical Balance, whereby the Specifick Gravities of ſeveral particular Bodies are actually found out. Some Account of the various Uſes of ſuch Enquiries.

PNEUMATICKS *illuſtrated by Experiments for the moſt part Tubular, being ſuch as were wont to be made before the Air-Pump was invented.*

19th DAY. THE ſeveral Phænomena of the Torricellian Experiment exhibited and explained. Other Experiments of the like Nature, with Fluids variouſly combin'd. Several Sorts of Barometers, Thermometers, and Hygroſcopes. The Preſſure of the Air ſhewn by Experiment to be different at different Altitudes from the Surface of the Earth.

20th—The Denſity and Spring of the Air proved by ſeveral ways to be as the Force which compreſſes it, and reciprocally as the Spaces into which it is compreſs'd. From hence an Enquiry is made into the Limits and State of the Atmoſphere.

21ſt—The Effects of the Weight and Spring of the Air in Syringes, Pumps, Siphons, poliſhed Plates, Cupping-Glaſſes, Suction: Reſpiration explained by artificial Lungs; That the Air may be ſo diſorder'd by a violent Impulſe, as to require Time to recover its Strength and Elaſticity again.

The more known Properties of the Air eſtabliſhed by the Air-Pump, and other Engines.

22d DAY. THE Air-Pump; the Inſtruments for Condenſing and Transferring of Air; their Fabrick, Operation, and Gages explained.

23d—A Parcel of Air weighed in the Balance; its Specifick Gravity to that of Water determined thereby; an artificial Storm, ſhewing that high Winds may make the Barometer ſink much and ſuddenly.

24th—The Weight, Preſſure, and Spring of the Air prov'd ſeveral ways; by the Senſe of Feeling; by breaking Glaſs Vials; by the Phænomena of Bladders, Glaſs-bubbles, Fountains; the Gardiner's Watering-Pot; the Diving-Bell, *&c.*

25th—The Torricellian Tube *in Vacuo*; Quickſilver raiſed to the uſual Height of the Weather-Glaſs, by the bare Spring of a little included Air; *Otto Gerick*'s Hemiſpheres; and that denſe Air has the ſame Advantage over common Air, as that has over a *Vacuum*.

The Ebullition of Liquors in *Vacuo*; the Quantity of Air contain'd in them; the Suſtentation of Fumes and Vapours; the Deſcent of Bodies *in Vacuo*.

The more hidden Properties of the Air conſider'd by the help of the like Engines.

26th DAY. THE Influence of the Air examin'd as to the Cauſes of Magnetiſm; the Elaſticity of Springs; the Cohæſion of the Parts of Matter; the Sphericity of the Drops of Fluids; the Aſcent of Liquors in capillary Tubes, and between Glaſs-Planes in the Curve of the Hyperbola, both by the Attractive and Repulſive Power of the Glaſs.

27th—The Influence of the Air, as to Sounds, Fire, and Flame; the Conſumption of Fuel; the firing of Gunpowder; the Effects of rarified, condenſed, and burnt Air upon the Life of Animals.

28th—A Piece of Phoſphorus *in Vacuo*; new Experiments concerning the Mercurial Phoſphori; Experiments concerning the Electricity of Bodies.

Every SUBSCRIBER *is to pay Three Guineas; One Guinea at the Time of Subſcription, and the Remainder, the Firſt Day of the* Courſe.

SUBSCRIPTIONS *are taken in at Mr.* Whiſton'*s, in* Great Ruſſel-Street; *and at Mr.* Hauksbee'*s, in* Crane-Court *in* Fleetſtreet; *where the Courſe is to be perform'd.*

Learning experimental philosophy in eighteenth-century London: prices and plan of the lectures organised by Francis Hauksbee and William Whiston. Catalogue no. 29.

30. Benjamin Martin (1705–1782)

A course of lectures in natural and experimental philosophy, geography and astronomy: in which the properties, affections, and phaenomena of natural bodies, hitherto discover'd, are exhibited and explain'd on the principles of the Newtonian philosophy. The whole confirmed by experiments, and illustrated with copper-plates. To which is added, an appendix, explaining all the characters, phrases, and difficult words, which occur in these lectures, and other treatises of this kind. By Benjamin Martin.

Reading, printed and sold by J. Newbery and C. Micklewright; also by Mess. Ware, Birt, Astley, Austen, Robinson, Dodsley and Needham; Mr. Fletcher; Mr. Thurlbourn; Mess. Ward and Chandler; Mr. Collins; Mr. Frederick; Mr. Craighton; and Mr. Wimpey, 1743
4°; 5 unsigned leaves a1 B-R4 B2

In the eighteenth century interest in natural philosophy extended well beyond the boundaries of learned societies and universities, as the popularity of public lectures shows. Using simple instruments such as balances, compasses and microscopes, but also more complicated apparatus such as air-pumps and later electrical machines, demonstrators would create dramatic effects to seize the attention of a growing paying public. In London such demonstrations were mostly carried out in coffee-houses; in the provinces, itinerant showmen would perform in assembly rooms for the gentry and nobility. A range of printed materials complemented the orality of these lectures: short announcements in newspapers, synopses of the courses, or volumes expanding on the matters presented.

Francis Hauksbee junior, the nephew of the first curator of experiments at the Royal Society, was an instrument maker who organised lectures at his shop in Crane Court, London. While he would handle the apparatus, William Whiston, former Lucasian professor of mathematics at Cambridge, from whence he had been banned for heterodoxy, would lecture. *A course of mechanical, magnetical, optical, hydrostatical and pneumatical experiments* does not have a proper title-page, and its date of publication, 1715, is conjectural. A three-page plan breaking down the contents of the course for each of its twenty-eight days was followed by a series of plates illus-

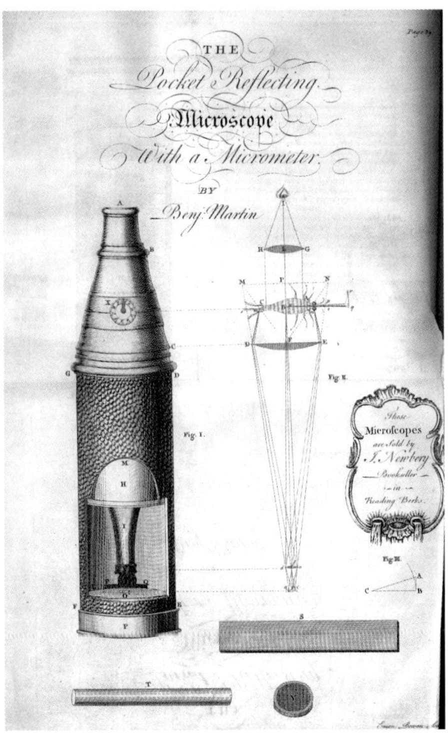

Buying microscopes from a bookseller in eighteenth-century England.
Catalogue no. 30.

trating both the apparatus and the results of some of the experiments. This publication was a hybrid between a condensed textbook and an extremely elaborate advertisement for both the lectures and Hauksbee's instruments. Details about the payment of the course, and a full-page advertisement of the whole range of Hauksbee's stock are very prominent. It is also possible, though, that those who attended the lectures would buy the book and attach the plates to their lecture notes.

By contrast, Benjamin Martin's *Course* was a faithful transcription of his twelve lectures. A school-teacher and an amazingly active entrepreneur, Martin exploited the booming commercial activities of eighteenth-century England, and a range of media, to popularise natural philosophy. He taught both in the provinces and in London, wrote an extraordinary number of successful publications, including books, pamphlets and a periodical, and made and sold instruments. In 1743 when this book was published, Martin was lecturing in Bristol and was in business with a number of booksellers in the south of the country. They financed the publication and would sell Martin's books as well as the instruments he used in his demonstrations. Martin regarded publishing as an effective way to establish his reputation as 'an illustrator of experimental philosophy', which he felt was threatened by bogus demonstrators using unreliable apparatus.

The book could be perused during the lectures, but above all it was to be read after them, to fix their contents in the mind and make sure that they became more than 'just a sublime and rational amusement'. Experiments were numbered, cross references between the text and the plates were given and an appendix with explanations of the essential terms and notions was added. It is difficult to say whether the book could be used also as a guide to performing experiments at home, but it is very likely that it reached a wider audience than the participants in the course. Martin was well aware that since 'knowledge had become a fashionable thing', women were a growing audience and he addressed them especially in his preface.

Taylor (1954; 1966); Millburn (1976); Guerlac (1981); Schaffer (1993); Clifton (1995); Walters (1997); Stewart (1999).

31. James Wood (1760–1839)

The elements of optics: designed for the use of students in the university. By James Wood. Third edition.

Cambridge, printed by J. Smith, printer to the university; and sold by J. Deighton, and J. Nicholson; and W. H. Lunn, 1811
250 p.

At the turn of the nineteenth century mathematics was becoming the dominant subject in Cambridge at the expense of both classical studies and natural philosophy. But even in the

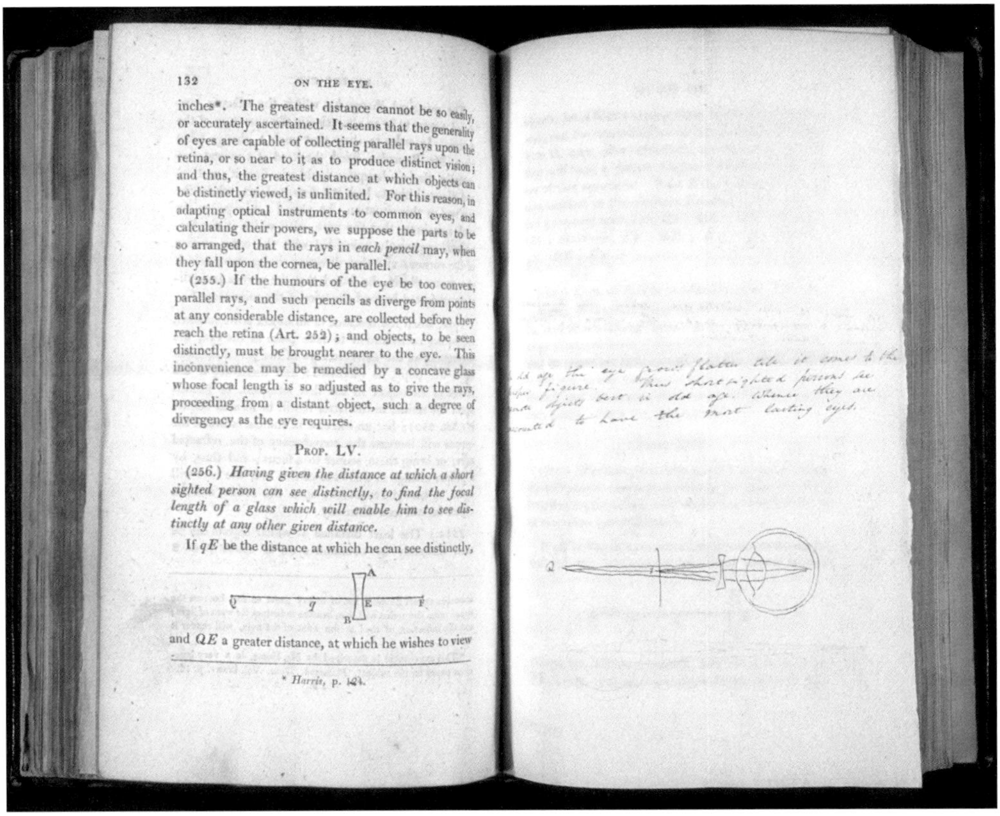

132 ON THE EYE.

inches*. The greatest distance cannot be so easily, or accurately ascertained. It seems that the generality of eyes are capable of collecting parallel rays upon the retina, or so near to it as to produce distinct vision; and thus, the greatest distance at which objects can be distinctly viewed, is unlimited. For this reason, in adapting optical instruments to common eyes, and calculating their powers, we suppose the parts to be so arranged, that the rays in *each pencil* may, when they fall upon the cornea, be parallel.

(255.) If the humours of the eye be too convex, parallel rays, and such pencils as diverge from points at any considerable distance, are collected before they reach the retina (Art. 252); and objects, to be seen distinctly, must be brought nearer to the eye. This inconvenience may be remedied by a concave glass whose focal length is so adjusted as to give the rays, proceeding from a distant object, such a degree of divergency as the eye requires.

PROP. LV.

(256.) *Having given the distance at which a short sighted person can see distinctly, to find the focal length of a glass which will enable him to see distinctly at any other given distance.*

If qE be the distance at which he can see distinctly, and QE a greater distance, at which he wishes to view

* *Harris*, p. 124.

Manuscript annotations in the interleaved copy of Wood's *Optics*.
Catalogue no. 31.

field of mathematics, the time available for original research was gradually shrinking, while teachers were busy writing or revising books for undergraduates. From the students' point of view, by contrast, a dramatic transformation was taking place, as the final oral examination in Latin was replaced by written papers which each student would sit over a period of three weeks, working from identical printed questions. This volume is one of the textbooks students used to prepare for these exams.

James Wood was a typical Cambridge don. He graduated in 1782 and became Master of St John's College in 1815; he never left Cambridge and accumulated a number of offices at the University. He published various textbooks which remained standard treatises for many years: his *Elements of algebra* (1795), for example, ran to sixteen editions; this work on optics, first published in 1798, to five. Although Wood concentrated on the mathematical aspects of optics, he included a long chapter on optical instruments. St John's College had at the time an observatory equipped with a range of optical instruments, and Wood donated a telescope, probably made by the firm of Dollond. However, he did not add to the book pictures of, or instructions on, the construction and uses of the microscopes, telescopes and magic lanterns which he discussed.

The copy in the Whipple collection is interleaved, that is, a blank leaf faces each of the printed leaves. The production of interleaved copies had been well-established since the early modern period: it allowed readers, especially artisans and professionals, to make additions and so to create working tools. In the case of textbooks, it provided students with an economical way of adding annotations and observations while reading. Booksellers such as Deighton and Nicholson in Cambridge, who based their business on catering for students, would produce a number of interleaved copies: another interleaved copy of Wood's *Optics* with annotations by the mathematician Miles Bland is in the Library of St John's College.

DNB; Gunther (1937); Gascoigne (1989); Warwick (1994); Searby (1997); McKitterick (1998); Topham (2000).

32. Science Schools, South Kensington

Practical instruction in physics.

[London] [1875]
[52 p.]

In 1872 the Department of Chemistry, Physics and Biology of the Schools of Mines was moved to South Kensington where in 1881 it became the Normal School of Science. Within the broader Victorian policy of boosting science education, South Kensington was to become a major site of learning and research. Teachers were encouraged to attend lectures at the School, and summer courses were arranged for those coming from the provinces. This volume, with the spine-title 'Physical Manipulations' contains a miscellany of instruction sheets. They include one set on sound, one loose

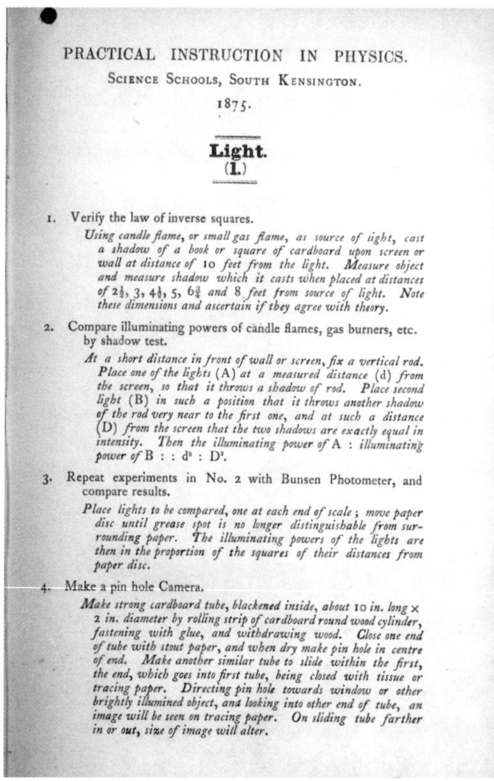

PRACTICAL INSTRUCTION IN PHYSICS.
SCIENCE SCHOOLS, SOUTH KENSINGTON.
1875.

Light.
(I.)

1. Verify the law of inverse squares.
   Using candle flame, or small gas flame, as source of light, cast a shadow of a book or square of cardboard upon screen or wall at distance of 10 *feet from the light. Measure object and measure shadow which it casts when placed at distances of* $2\frac{1}{2}$, 3, $4\frac{1}{2}$, 5, $6\frac{3}{4}$ *and* 8 *feet from source of light. Note these dimensions and ascertain if they agree with theory.*
2. Compare illuminating powers of candle flames, gas burners, etc. by shadow test.
   At a short distance in front of wall or screen, fix a vertical rod. Place one of the lights (A) *at a measured distance* (d) *from the screen, so that it throws a shadow of rod. Place second light* (B) *in such a position that it throws another shadow of the rod very near to the first one, and at such a distance* (D) *from the screen that the two shadows are exactly equal in intensity. Then the illuminating power of* A : *illuminating power of* B : : d^2 : D^2.
3. Repeat experiments in No. 2 with Bunsen Photometer, and compare results.
   Place lights to be compared, one at each end of scale; move paper disc until grease spot is no longer distinguishable from surrounding paper. The illuminating powers of the lights are then in the proportion of the squares of their distances from paper disc.
4. Make a pin hole Camera.
   Make strong cardboard tube, blackened inside, about 10 *in. long* × 2 *in. diameter by rolling strip of cardboard round wood cylinder, fastening with glue, and withdrawing wood. Close one end of tube with stout paper, and when dry make pin hole in centre of end. Make another similar tube to slide within the first, the end, which goes into first tube, being closed with tissue or tracing paper. Directing pin hole towards window or other brightly illumined object, and looking into other end of tube, an image will be seen on tracing paper. On sliding tube farther in or out, size of image will alter.*

Learning physics in nineteenth-century London.
Catalogue no. 32.

sheet of chemistry, two different sets on light, one of which is dated 1875, two different sets on heat, one set on electricity and magnetism. All the sheets have the same structure: the assigned task—to make an apparatus, to determine experimentally certain values, or to test an instrument—is printed in roman type; brief instructions follow in italic. There are no images. A little hole on each sheet shows that students were supposed to gather their own sets, possibly attaching hand-written notes. The course on Experimental Physics was taught by Dr. Frederick Guthrie (1833–1886) and it is likely that these instruction sheets were part of his course.

After receiving a chemical doctorate in Germany, Guthrie came back to England and started to teach at South Kensington in 1869. Experimental teaching in laboratories was still rare in England, and Guthrie imported from Germany a very practical mode of teaching physics, which involved the construction of the apparatus by students themselves. These instruction sheets, a little known type of printed material related to instruments, allow us to see this new pedagogical system in action.

This copy belonged to George Mathews Whipple, Robert Whipple's father, who made a successful career at the Kew Observatory and in 1876 became superintendent. In 1871 he received a B.Sc. from the University of London, where he subsequently became assistant examiner in natural philosophy. In the years 1879–82 and 1884–89 he held the same position at the Science Schools of South Kensington.

DNB; Turner, D. M. (1981); Argles (1964); Anderson (1995).

33. Charles Polydor Francotte (1851–1916)

Manuel de technique microscopique applicable a l'histologie, l'anatomie comparée, l'embryologie et la botanique. Par P. Francotte.

Bruxelles, J. Lebègue et C.ie. [1886]
vii, 433 p.

In the second half of the nineteenth century the community of people practising microscopy was large and varied. The range of publications dealing with microscopy was correspondingly diverse. University professors would increasingly report the results of their research in academic periodicals, though publishing books containing new results was still common at the end of the century. The market was saturated with up-to-date editions of textbooks for students and with technical manuals; authors of elementary books would bank on the fascination which microscopical objects never failed to exert on a wide audience, including children.

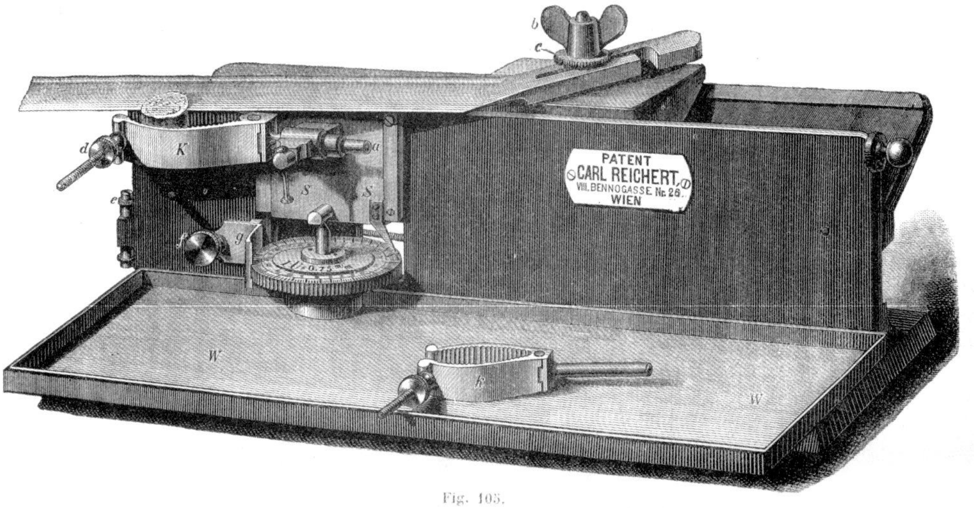

A microtome to slice specimens: an exciting new tool for anatomical research in Charles Polydor Francotte's manual.
Catalogue no. 33.

Charles P. Francotte was a professor at the University of Brussels and a member of the Belgian Microscopical Society; he researched the embryological development of frogs, and contributed to the improvement of the microtome, a tool for slicing specimens which revolutionised anatomical investigations. His volume on microscopical techniques, which included a discussion of microtomes, was very up-to-date. But in the preface Francotte made clear that he was writing primarily with an audience of isolated scholars in mind. While those working in a university or in other scientific laboratories could enjoy state-of-the-art equipment and would have access to the current literature, there were researchers who could not take advantage of such facilities. Francotte intended to provide them with the means to carry out individual investigations. After a detailed discussion of dissecting methods and microscopical techniques, he selected a number of exercises which would make a beginner familiar with matter usually discussed in more complicated anatomical and histological treatises. He also added brief pieces of advice on how to carry out original research and a comprehensive list of books and periodicals in the field.

This volume helps us appreciate the existence of a wide non-academic audience actively pursuing microscopical research even at the end of the nineteenth century. These readers, possibly with medical backgrounds, were able to follow the latest technical improvements and eager to contribute to the development of natural research. This is a presentation copy which Francotte sent to Frank Crisp (catalogue no. 50).

Debus (1968); Bracegirdle (1978); Turner, G. L'E. (1980); Bennett (1989); Gooday (1991).

Books for recreation

Throughout the centuries a great number of books dealt with instruments as objects of entertainment. This is meant in a broad sense. It includes, for example, the pleasure which rotating a volvelle was supposed to produce in readers of a sixteenth-century astronomical book, and the entertainment which the genre of the 'rational recreations' provided to generations of readers between the sixteenth and the nineteenth century. The tactile delight which manipulating objects could provoke has always been part of the fascination for instruments; books could enhance it by providing readers with instructions about how to delve further into the mysteries of nature. But boundaries between 'serious' learning and entertainment, proper and improper amusement changed over the centuries; fun became appropriate only insofar as it was conducive to knowledge, and instruments creating illusions came to be regarded with suspicion. Towards the mid-nineteenth century, as scientific apparatus permeated the lives of many, fairs and international exhibitions of instruments, followed by publications and catalogues, combined popular entertainment with celebrations of national pride and scientific values.

34. Giovanni Paolo Gallucci (1538–1621?)

Speculum uranicum in quo vera loca tum octavae sphaerae, tum septem planetarum mira facilitate ad quodlibet datum tempus ex prutenicarum ratione colliguntur, unà cum regulis fabricandi duodecim coeli domicilia ex Regiomontano, & Alcabitio, & dirigendi significatores ad promissores sequentes. Io. Paulo Gallucio auctore.

Venetiis, apud Damianum Zenarium, 1593
2°; †4 A-L4

In late sixteenth-century Venice the offspring of ruling families would usually receive a private education. Giovanni Paolo Gallucci earned his living teaching mathematics and rhetoric to young noble-

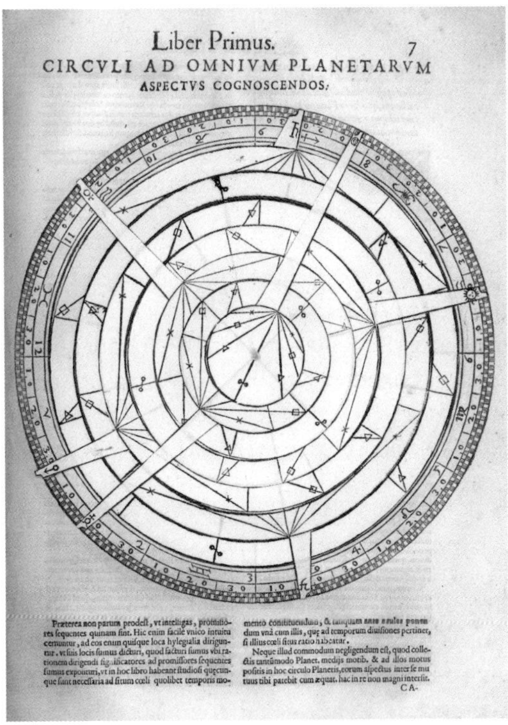

Taking pleasure in learning astronomy: a complicated volvelle to rotate in Giovanni Paolo Gallucci's book.
Catalogue no. 34.

men, and publishing books, most of which were meant to make knowledge accessible to a lay audience. For example, he translated into Italian, and commented on, several Latin works. He believed that the more varied and sophisticated the iconographical apparatus of a book, the greater its pedagogical value. In addition to engravings and woodcuts, Gallucci often resorted to a more complicated form of visual aid: moveable discs mounted in several layers and sewn on a page. These discs—now called volvelles—were relatively common in astronomical books because they made calculations easier. More generally, illustrations with moveable parts or flaps were widely used in publications produced for the growing and varied audience of non-academic readers. For example, popular anatomical broadsheets and manuals of rhetoric would include some of these illustrations, which transformed a book into a multifunctional tool.

In his *Speculum uranicum*, which explained how to find the positions of the planets, Gallucci expressed concern that learning astronomy could be a dry and daunting job. To help readers, he had taken the greatest care to arrange the page sequence so that all the data concerning a particular planet would be found on pages facing each other. He also emphasised that he had put in numerous volvelles to add an element of pleasure: following the neoplatonist philosopher Marsilio Ficino, Gallucci argued that nothing was more amusing than circular images: not only did the mind enjoy itself in contemplating and manipulating circles, but the body and its health could also benefit from these activities.

That this volume was not just a useful handbook but also a beautiful and precious object, aiming to provide aesthetic pleasure, was already announced by its magnificent title-page, which was produced by the well-known engraver Giacomo Franco. In aristocratic hands this book could serve several functions: it could be read and handled to learn astronomy, but it could also be shown, precisely in the same way as many of the astronomical instruments which noblemen collected would be displayed in their cabinets to provide entertainment.

Lindberg (1979); Gingerich (1993); Bolzoni (1995); Ernst (1998).

35. Accademia del Cimento (1657–1667)

Saggi di naturali esperienze fatte nell'Accademia del Cimento sotto la protezione del Serenissimo principe Leopoldo di Toscana e descritte dal segretario di essa Accademia.

In Firenze, per Giuseppe Cocchini, 1666
2°; 4 unsigned leaves †4 A-2L4 *6 1 unsigned leaf

Since the Renaissance, the family of the Medici, rulers of Florence, had actively cultivated their public image as patrons of the arts. In the seventeenth century the Grand Duke Ferdinando II and his brother Leopoldo extended their support to natural investigations, including experi-

Experiments to entertain a duke: the portrait of Ferdinando II on the frontispiece of the *Saggi* of the Accademia del Cimento. Catalogue no. 35.

ments done with recently invented instruments such as the barometer and the thermometer. In particular, they promoted informal gatherings of virtuosi during which nature would be tested in various ways; the Academy of the Cimento originated from such meetings. Experimental activities in the Academy stemmed from, and remained close to, a popular form of court entertainment in which the Grand Duke would propose to his courtiers a puzzle or question arising from some amazing natural phenomenon and would expect witty explanations of it. Instruments increased the amusement.

To give full visibility to their new patronage, the Medici encouraged the publication of the *Saggi,* a collection of the academicians' most interesting experiments. To avoid possible conflicts among them and to celebrate the Academy as a collective body, neither the names of those who had carried out the experiments, nor a theoretical framework were provided. More than bearing testimony to the development of a coherent experimental philosophy, the *Saggi,* written in beautiful prose by Lorenzo Magalotti, became a tangible symbol of the Medici's inclination for intellectual recreations.

No arrangement was made with booksellers to market the book; it was sent out, rather, as a gift to a list of people which the Medici drew up: rulers, aristocrats and famous scholars who could enjoy its graceful prose, be amused by the description of the *esperienze* and above all appreciate the magnanimity of Leopoldo and Ferdinando II. The Grand Duke's magnificent engraved portrait served this purpose well. But making the book proved difficult. The printer Cocchini, who was not used to books with illustrations, was slow and sloppy; proof reading was poor. Illustrations of the instruments were abundant but, together with the general decoration and lay-out, not particularly good; contemporary readers complained that the index was of little use. The volume's circulation was also problematic: while readers with an interest in experimental philosophy, but of lower social status, hardly had the opportunity to see the book until a second edition in 1691, in the 1730s many of the eight hundred copies of the first were still sitting in wraps in the Grand Duke's library.

Pagnini (1942); Middleton (1971; 1975); Galluzzi (1981); Biagioli (1992); Tribby (1994).

36. Jacques Ozanam (1640–1717?)

Récréations mathématiques et physiques, qui contiennent plusieurs problèmes utiles & agréables, d'arithmetique, de geometrie, d'optique, de gnomonique, de cosmographie, de mecanique, de pyrotechnie, & de physique. Avec un traité nouveau des horloges elementaires. Par M. Ozanam.

A Amsterdam, chez George Gallet, 1696
8°; *7 A-Z8 2A-2P8

In late seventeenth-century France the demand for mathematical training was on the increase, as more would-be army and navy officers as well as merchants were required to master basic mathematics and the use of instruments than ever before. Practical mathematics was also part of the standard curriculum provided by Jesuit colleges, and together with the manipulation of instruments was also becoming a source of entertainment in salons and academies, where noble virtuosi, including women, would meet.

Jacques Ozanam was a private tutor of mathematics: most of his publications were closely linked to his teaching. In addition to books on specific topics such as perspective and surveying, he published a five-volume *Cours de mathématiques.* The *Récréations mathématiques et physiques*, first published in 1694, were intended to provide a wider range of problems than could fit into the already bulky *Cours.* Though

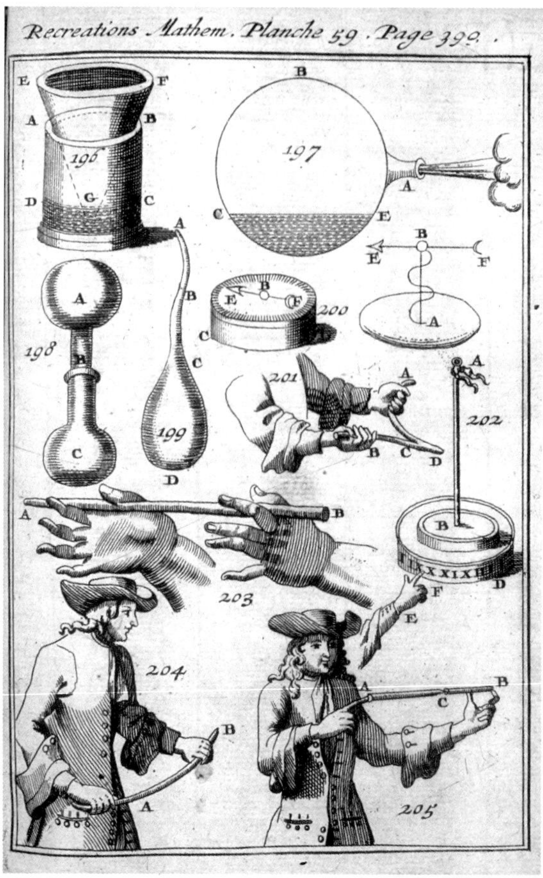

How to find water with a stick and other amusing activities with water in Ozanam's volume of rational recreations.
Catalogue no. 36.

formulated as problems, Ozanam's recreations were meant to amuse as well as instruct. The book had many editions throughout the eighteenth century.

In the preface Ozanam firmly placed his problems within the long-standing tradition of mathematical games going back to ancient Egyptian enigmas. In addition to mathematics, the *Récréations* also included problems of dialling, pyrotechnics, mechanics, optics and hydraulics, the solution of which required knowledge of instruments such as sundials, lenses, balances and compasses. Tricks and games to be played with these objects were popular in seventeenth-century public spectacles and private parties. Ozanam's aim was to explain how the various devices worked so that spectators could enjoy the illusion without being deceived by it.

Overall the *Récréations* might be regarded as a heterogeneous publication. The discussion of mathematics is at times very technical, while the section on physics covers a range of topics as diverse as methods for finding water with a stick, recipes to make a magic powder and the recent invention of barometers. As Ozanam wrote, these games could bring mathematics and other sciences within the reach of a variety of readers: they were the best way to teach young people; they could amuse the elderly; both rich and poor would enjoy them; and they were appropriate for both men and women.

Schaaf (1981); Brockliss (1987); Stroup (1990); Stafford (1994).

37. Joachim Dalencé (ca 1640–1707?)

*Traittez des barométres, thermométres, et notiométres, ou hygrométres. Par Mr. D***.*

A Amsterdam, chez Henry Wetstein, 1688
12°; *6 A-E12 F-G6

Thermometers and barometers were experimental philosophers' favourite instruments, but they soon became popular in wider circles: increasingly, aristocrats and gentlemen were keen to learn how to use them. In the process, instruments acquired new functions. For example, in addition to studying the nature of the void, barometers were used to perform the

Barometers in a seventeenth-century country landscape.
Catalogue no. 37.

socially more important act of forecasting the weather; they soon appeared in many households. Instrument makers marketing fancy barometers, and books such as the *Traittez*, further promoted the new fashion.

Dalencé, who withdrew his name from the title-page of this book, worked as an agent for the King of France, buying books and art objects for the royal collections. This put him in contact with the world of scientific academies such as the Royal Society and the Académie des Sciences, and with a broader network of gentlemen. In a review in the *Journal des Sçavans*, one of the first periodicals devoted to promoting natural knowledge outside the circles of virtuosi and philosophers, the *Traittez* was recommended as 'useful for all those who are starting to study physics without a teacher'. In the preface, Dalencé claimed that if readers followed his instructions in assembling the instruments, they would be rewarded with the ability to forecast 'changes of air'.

The *Traittez* was a relatively cheap publication—the 1688 edition was in duodecimo and the 1691 edition, though in quarto, is not luxurious. One of the strongest selling points must have been its wealth of plates of barometers and thermometers. The emphasis was on the diversity of decoration and shapes, and variety of genteel settings for their use, rather than specific details of construction. The text provided explanations of the experiments to be carried out, but lacked a broader discussion of their significance. The instrument maker Hubin, the 'King's enameller' who ran a successful workshop in Paris and was a pioneer in marketing instruments to a wide audience, is mentioned at the end of this volume as one of the most reliable and knowledgeable craftsmen.

Middleton (1964); Goodison (1969); Daumas (1972); Taton (1981); Licoppe (1996); Turner, A. (1998); Golinski (1999).

38. William Hooper (fl. 1770)

Rational recreations, in which the principles of numbers and natural philosophy are clearly and copiously elucidated, by a series of easy, entertaining, interesting experiments. Among which are all those commonly performed with the cards. By W. Hooper.

London, printed for L. Davis; J. Robson; B. Law; and G. Robinson, 1774
8°; 4 volumes

By presenting his recreations in the form of 'problems', Ozanam (catalogue no. 36) conveyed the message that games could have a serious, pedagogical function. A century later William Hooper, whose four-volume *Rational recreations* drew extensively from Ozanam, removed the word 'problem' from his book. It dealt with magnetism, optics and pneumatics, and each section opened with basic definitions and a description of the most

How to make artificial magnets and provide amusement with them.
Catalogue no. 38.

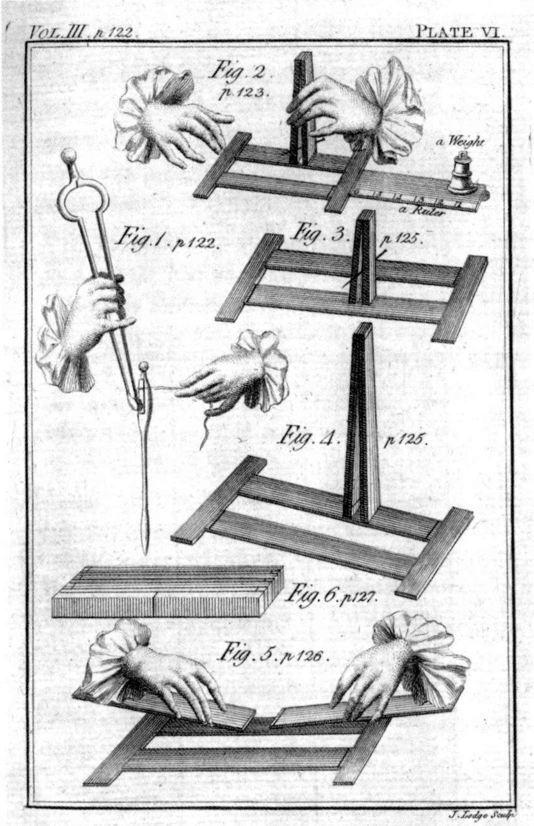

important experimental apparatus. But Hooper meant to provide ready-made amusements rather than instructive recreations; practical tips about how to perform games outweighed explanations of causes and effects. Lengthy tables of contents with summaries of the recreations complemented each volume and made it easy for readers to select and perform their favourite games in the order of their choice. The 'conversive statue', for example, which was based on a mixture of optical and acoustical devices, was one of the tricks which could have a great impact on the audience.

In the eighteenth century experimental philosophy was recommended as a family pastime for its instructive and moral value, but it had to compete with other equally popular and less enlightening diversions, for example card games. Contemporaries were increasingly concerned about the boundaries between proper and improper entertainment: cards, for example, could be used as learning aids, but were perceived as dangerously close to the realm of tricks, frauds and deceits. Hooper included a large number of card games in his volumes. His work was challenged on the grounds that these recreations were rather about how to be a successful conjuror than about how to perform an experiment.

Although some people stressed the apparatus' potential proximity to trickery and magic, marketing the paraphernalia with which to perform such recreations was becoming sophisticated. The famous London instrument maker George Adams (catalogue no. 46), for example, published a catalogue specifically entitled *A catalogue of the instruments and machines for performing the several experiments in the 'Rational recreations' by W. Hooper.* Adams claimed that his instruments were made under Hooper's direct inspection.

Secord (1985); Anderson, Burnet and Gee (1990); Stafford (1994); Fara (1995); Hankins and Silverman (1995).

39. Thomas Dick (1774–1857)

The telescope and microscope. By Thomas Dick.

London, The Religious Tract Society [1851]
192 p.

40. *How to choose a microscope. By a demonstrator. With eighty illustrations.*

London, Hardwicke and Bogue, 1876
32 p.

As control over leisure time became part of the nineteenth-century strategy for imposing a strict morality and an industrious life-style on the working masses, reading emerged as one of the safest and most appropriate pastimes. Religious associations encouraged it among all classes.

Drawing on increasing literacy and at the same time promoting it among wider sections of the population, the evangelical Religious Tract Society, founded in 1799, was one of the most active centres for the production and distribution of religious material. Hundreds of thousands of tracts were circulated. By the mid-nineteenth century the competition from cheap non-religious publications became fiercer and the Society widened the range of its output. Controversies about the suitability of science for infusing religious zeal gave way to a more positive attitude, and the sanctification of science for evangelical consumption prevailed. Astronomy, natural history and history provided the most popular topics of the volumes included in the *Monthly series*, which comprised booklets of the standard length of 192 pages. Meant to reach a wide working-class audience, the style of these volumes was simple and their size allowed readers to carry them around easily. The cost was kept low, but the fact that the volumes were available in two bindings at different prices—six pence for the paper covers and ten for the cloth with gilt edges—meant that the publisher was banking on a varied audience. It is likely that more middle-class than

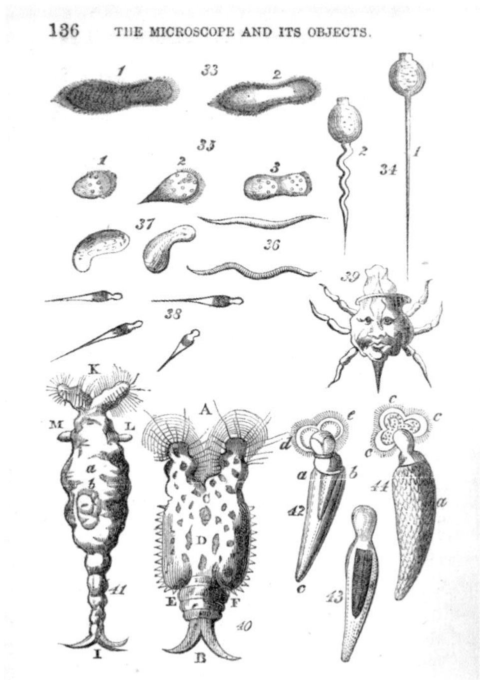

Microscopical wonder: an animalcule with a human face.
Catalogue no. 39.

working-class families actually bought the volumes, but through the expanding system of libraries they probably reached a wider readership.

Drawing on the centuries-long celebration of the telescope and the microscope as the best means to show the beauty and glory of the divine creation, Thomas Dick provided his readers with explanations of the construction and history of these instruments. A teacher and the founder of a people's library, Dick contributed several volumes to the *Monthly series*; in *The telescope and the microscope*, he showed how by contemplating the sky and minute creatures instruction and recreation could be mingled with deep Christian devotion.

Partly for their theological implications, natural historical investigations remained very popular in Victorian England: microscopes were the main tool both for carrying out field research and for enjoying indoor recreation. As the anonymous author of *How to choose a microscope* wrote, the purchase of a microscope was an important step in the practice of microscopy. The book belonged to a series of popular books of science produced by the London publishing house Bogue and Hardwick, which also produced, if for a different segment of the market, the *Monthly microscopical journal*. Hardwick had been an important scientific publisher, well known for the periodical *Science gossip*. At his death, Bogue bought the firm and continued to cater for the varied audience of people interested in science. Sold at a price ranging between two and five shillings, *How to choose a microscope* and the other volumes in the series addressed beginners and young people. Although the series included titles such as *Half-hours with the stars*, it mainly comprised books on natural history. Readers without a scientific training or, as the author wrote, a scientific friend, would find in the book reliable information. The thirty-two pages described in some detail but with simple words the various microscopes available on the market. No discussion of optical theory was added and the title-page reference to eighty illustrations was a con: eighty numbered images were crammed into just two plates. A brief chapter on other useful tools and some advice about how much the readers should expect to pay for their chosen instruments concluded the book.

DNB; Altick (1957); Allen (1994); Bennett (1989); Brock (1989); Gooday (1991); Topham (1992); Fyfe (2000).

41. Science and Art Department of the Committee of Council on Education

Catalogue of the special loan collection of scientific apparatus at the South Kensington Museum. 1876. Third edition.

London, printed by George E. Eyre and William Spottiswoode, for Her Majesty's Stationery Office, 1877
lviii, 1084 p.

In the second half of the nineteenth century, following the great success of the Great Exhibition of 1851, going to temporary expositions became a popular form of recreation in European and American cities. Millions of visitors enjoyed the variety of commodities on display, among which

A symbol of triumphant science and technology: the locomotive engine 'Rocket' on display in the section 'Prime movers' at the Special Loan Collection of Scientific Apparatus, 1876. Catalogue no. 41.

"The Rocket," described under No. 1934.

industrial machinery and apparatus embodied the scientific progress they celebrated. Some of these exhibitions gave way to more permanent scientific and industrial museums. In London, the Museum of Industrial Art in South Kensington (now the Victoria and Albert Museum) was built around a nucleus of objects from the Great Exhibition. For some years its collection of scientific instruments was neglected, but as concerns arose about the scientific instruction of the general public, it became clear that they might be put to use.

In 1874 a Committee, including some of the best-known scientists and engineers, launched the project of a Special Loan Collection of Scientific Apparatus, which opened in 1876 with five thousand objects on display. The organisers stressed the differences between this and other, much more commercially oriented, international exhibitions. The aim of the Special Loan was mostly educational, and items were displayed according to a generic classification, not by nationality. Historic instruments from various private and public collections as well as relics of famous scientists were also exhibited, while teaching apparatus was gathered in a special section. A number of activities complemented the show, including a series of conferences and free evening lectures for the general public: topics were as varied as: 'Davy's and Faraday's apparatus', 'Astronomical instruments' and 'Photographic printing processes'. As one of the organisers put it, the exhibition was meant to provide young men with a useful pastime: they would learn by seeing instruments instead of just reading about them in books. But the exhibition was accompanied by a profusion of publications.

A small handbook was produced for visitors, and both the conferences and the evening lectures were published. The comprehensive catalogue of the collection was very successful, with two expanded English editions and translations into French and German. It had few illustrations and the general public probably did not buy it as a souvenir, but it complemented the rational recreations which a wide range of visitors could enjoy. Those with a professional interest in instruments, including makers, could find information here about state-of-the-art apparatus, teachers could focus on the educational sections, and amateurs could appreciate the variety of historical instruments, exciting brand-new technological devices, as well as simpler instruments for domestic amusement.

Brain (1994); Anderson (1995); Auerbach (1999).

3

Marketing Instruments

As the production of instruments diversified and the market for them grew over the centuries, advertising became an essential aspect of the business. Print was an effective way of reaching a large public and making manufacturers' expertise and output widely known. By presenting a range of printed advertisements of instruments, this section focuses on an important chapter in the relations between science and commerce.

In the early modern period, advertisement was mainly informal, often a simple reference to an instrument maker included in a book on that instrument (Bryden 1992). Later, instrument makers followed the advertising strategies developed in the book trade, and catalogues of instruments started to be produced. The growing popularity of instruments in eighteenth-century navigation and surveying led to substantial changes in their production, for example, strict guild regulations gave way to a system in which makers could sell a wide range of items. At the same time a consumption-driven culture spread and advertising strategies diversified. Trade cards, broadsheets with information about the latest inventions, sale-catalogues, advertisements in newspapers and the periodical press were favourite media of instrument makers.

Diversification intensified with the emergence of mass production and consumption in the nineteenth century: advertising became an increasingly prominent activity in every business, and instrument makers adapted to the new condition. By the middle of the century the long tradition of decorated trade cards was combined with that of simpler price lists of instruments to make those bulky and heavily illustrated catalogues which any decent maker would produce to appeal to both professional scientists and amateurs. Sometimes these volumes included a great deal of technical information and even competed with textbooks (Brenni 1989). A distinction between research-oriented and market-oriented makers was also drawn in the nineteenth century. However, even firms dealing exclusively with scientists, such as the Cambridge Scientific Instrument Company, would develop sophisticated forms of advertisement to stimulate sales, including postcards and vigorous campaigns in the specialised press. The aim of publicising the products on offer, though, could be counterbalanced by concerns about keeping certain aspects of their manufacture confidential. A further confirmation, if one be needed, of the tensions between publicity and secrecy in twentieth-century science.

42. Edmund Gunter (1581–1626)

The description and use of the sector. The crosse-staffe and other instruments. For such as are studious of mathematicall practise.

At London, printed by William Jones and are to be sold by Edmund Weaver, 1624

4°; A-T4 a-z4 2a-2d4

Early modern books on instruments generally included illustrations, and often a brief reference to the maker who was able to provide the instrument would be added to the main picture of the volume. Together with references to instrument makers scattered in the text, these are examples of what has been called 'informal advertising'. As new editions of the book were published over the years, such references would usually be updated. But sometimes the alteration to be made on the copperplate was too expensive and time-consuming: names of makers could appear well after their death.

Gunter, the professor of astronomy at Gresham College, published this book only after it had already circulated as a manuscript for sixteen years. It became a classic and went through three subsequent editions before 1653. The first edition was produced in a number of variant issues, because several booksellers joined the enterprise at a later stage and parts of the book were added. A range of title-pages and anomalous copies survive, a clear example of the 'instability' which characterised early modern books. Even the advertisement of the makers of the sector which appears on the plate illustrating the instrument varied. The names of Elias Allen and John Thompson are present in all the variants. Since they produced the same instruments in different materials, the former specialising in brass, the latter in wood, they are often coupled together. In some variants of the book the advertisement included their addresses. The

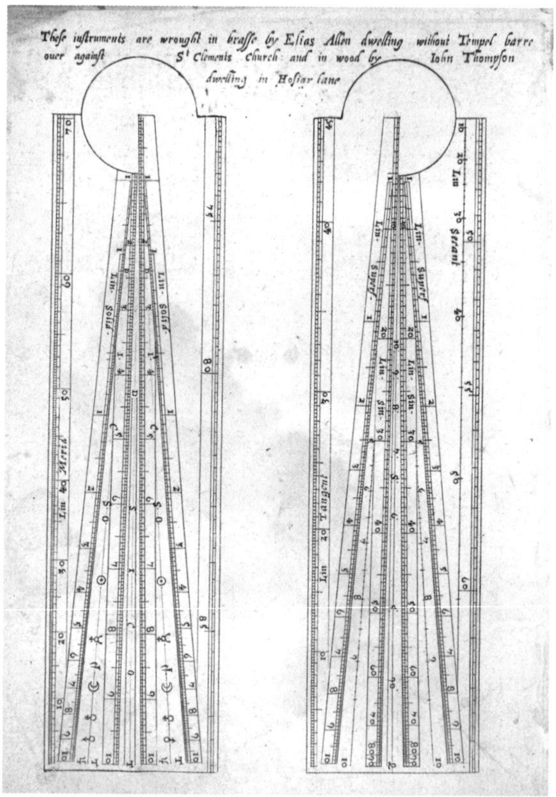

Engraving of Edmund Gunter's sector with the advertisement of the London instrument makers Elias Allen and John Thompson
Catalogue no. 42.

name of the instrument maker and bookseller Nathaniel Goss was included in one. Although makers, booksellers and authors usually worked in close association, we do not know if in this case the changes were the result of negotiations between printer and makers, or if the author was aware of such deals.

Taylor (1954); Pollard and Redgrave (1986); Bryden (1992; 1999); Clifton (1995).

43. Joseph Moxon (1627–1691)

Mechanick dyalling: teaching any man, though of an ordinary capacity and unlearned in the mathematicks, to draw a true sun-dyal on any given plane, however scituated: only with the help of a straight ruler and a pair of compasses; and without any arithmetical calculation. By Joseph Moxon.

London, printed for Joseph Moxon, 1668
4°; A-G4

Joseph Moxon was famous for his globes. He also published several books, including an important *Mathematical dictionary*, and developed close links with the virtuosi of the Royal Society. Appointed Hydrographer, that is map printer and seller, to the King, he became an FRS in 1678. He had a particular interest in printing techniques, made types and wrote a book on printing. In his shop he sold books, globes and maps, as well as other mathematical instruments, which he made mainly by pasting printed paper versions of the instruments onto wood: he was the first to market such paper instruments in London.

At the end of his *Meckanick dyalling*, Moxon inserted a five-page catalogue of the globes, maps, instruments and books which he sold. Prices were added too. Most, but not all of the listed books were by him: he boasted that he could provide a range of mathematical books at the lowest price. Book catalogues were among the first trade

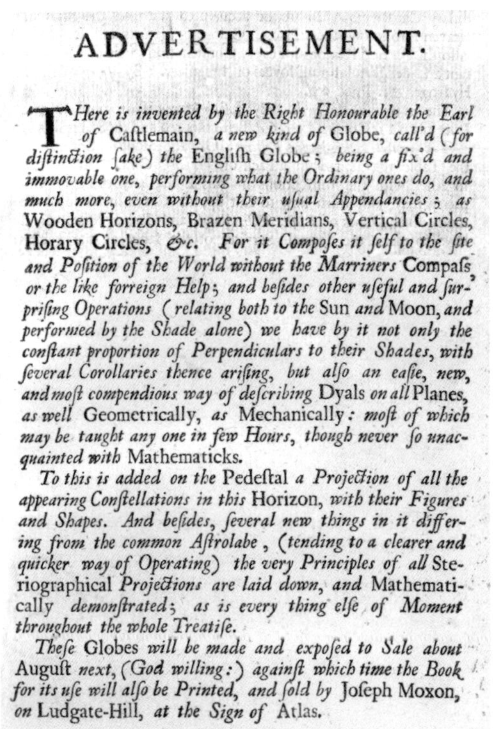
ADVERTISEMENT.

There is invented by the Right Honourable the Earl of Caſtlemain, *a new kind of* Globe, *call'd (for diſtinction ſake) the* Engliſh Globe; *being a fix'd and immovable one, performing what the Ordinary ones do, and much more, even without their uſual Appendancies; as* Wooden Horizons, Brazen Meridians, Vertical Circles, Horary Circles, *&c. For it Compoſes it ſelf to the ſite and Poſition of the World without the Marriners* Compaſs, *or the like forreign Help; and beſides other uſeful and ſurpriſing Operations (relating both to the* Sun *and* Moon, *and performed by the Shade alone) we have by it not only the conſtant proportion of Perpendiculars to their Shades, with ſeveral Corollaries thence ariſing, but alſo an eaſie, new, and moſt compendious way of deſcribing* Dyals *on all* Planes, *as well* Geometrically, *as* Mechanically: *moſt of which may be taught any one in few Hours, though never ſo unacquainted with* Mathematicks.

To this is added on the Pedeſtal *a Projection of all the appearing Conſtellations in this* Horizon, *with their Figures and Shapes. And beſides, ſeveral new things in it differing from the common Aſtrolabe, (tending to a clearer and quicker way of Operating) the very Principles of all* Steriographical *Projections are laid down, and* Mathematically *demonſtrated; as is every thing elſe of Moment throughout the whole Treatiſe.*

Theſe Globes *will be made and expoſed to Sale about* Auguſt *next, (God willing:) againſt which time the Book for its uſe will alſo be Printed, and ſold by* Joſeph Moxon, *on* Ludgate-Hill, *at the Sign of* Atlas.

Advertisement for the 'English globe' in Joseph Moxon's work on dialling.
Catalogue no. 43.

catalogues ever produced. Given Moxon's familiarity with book production, it was easy for him to expand the catalogues of the books he sold to include all the goods in which he traded. These included sets of astronomical playing cards and anatomical sheets, that is, series of engravings of the human body pasted together so that by lifting flaps successive stages of an anatomical dissection would be revealed.

In a separate section following the catalogue, Moxon also advertised an 'English globe' recently designed by the Earl of Castlemain. Moxon hoped to be able to market it in the near future together with a handbook for its use. In reality, the book had already been written, but the imprisonment of Castlemain as a suspected Jesuit had delayed publication. Moxon continued to promote the globe which, unlike most others produced at the time, was fixed and inclined for the latitude of London. To call it an 'English globe' was at the same time a faithful description of the object and an effective advertisement.

DNB; Taylor (1954); Anderson, Burnett and Gee (1990); Clifton (1995); Bryden (1997a); Bennett (1998); Johns (1998); Carlino (1999).

44. John Yarwell (1648–1712). Trade card

If the odd reference to a maker in a book was an example of informal advertisement, printed trade cards gave a maker the opportunity to announce his production formally. The main feature of cards was an image: at first it was the same as the shop-sign; later, illustrations of the goods became more popular. Made in various sizes, trade cards could be of different shapes. Makers would give them to prospective customers or paste them on instrument boxes. Often the engraving would be re-used—for example, sent to a newspaper to be printed—so that the advertisement reached a wider audience. The popularity of trade cards in the eighteenth-century English instrument market shows the increasing commercial pressure on makers and their need to beat competition by reaching out to prospective customers. Trade cards would generally include only a few technical details, except when makers could claim novelties in the production. Usually, they would bank on the impression which images of the instruments and other decorative elements conveyed.

John Yarwell was a member of the Spectacle-Makers Company and became renowned for his ability in grinding lenses and making optical instruments. These could appeal to a diverse audience; the market for optical instruments was wider than that for mathematical instruments. We do not know who engraved Yarwell's card, but compared to other contemporary cards, the arrangement of the instruments is remarkably neat. It has been suggested that the image of the man using a telescope was made after the portrait of the celebrated Polish astronomer Hevelius in his *Machinae coelestis* (catalogue no. 12). Only the readers of Hevelius' work would have been able to appreciate this reference, but it would certainly have enhanced their confidence in Yarwell's competence.

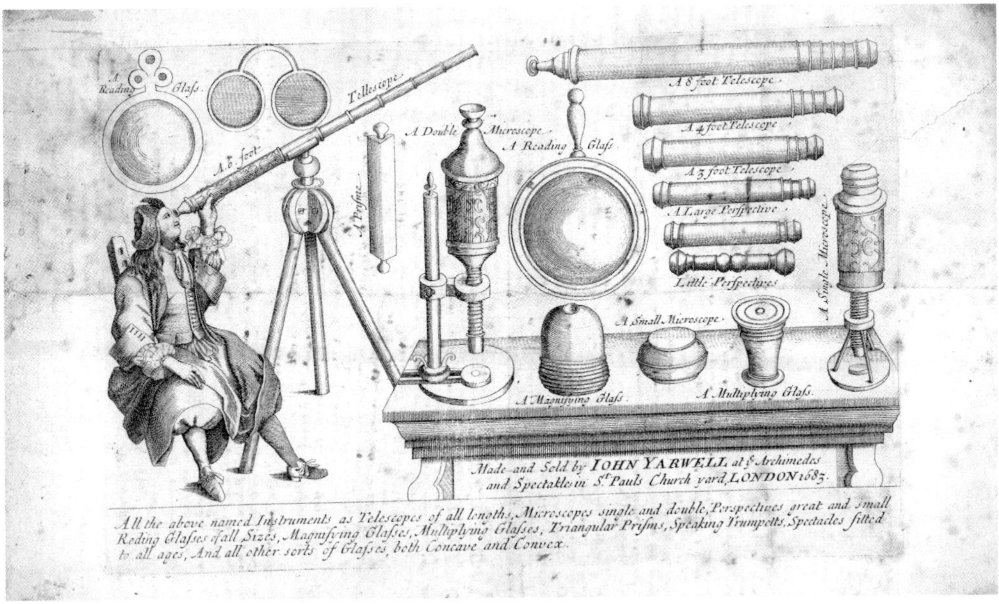

Trade card of the eighteenth-century optician John Yarwell.
Catalogue no. 44.

Trade cards were very fragile and ephemeral: very few copies of Yarwell's cards are extant. The copy in the Whipple Museum is particularly interesting because it belonged to Isaac Newton, who copied onto the back some passages from an edition of the *Fables* attributed to the Latin scholar Gaius Julius Hyginus. Whipple appreciated the importance of this very remarkable piece in his collection and wrote an article about it.

Heal (1925); Whipple (1951); Taylor (1954); Calvert (1971); Crawforth (1985); Bryden (1992); Clifton (1995).

45. Broadsheet, ca 1770

In eighteenth-century England itinerant practitioners performing experiments became part of the urban, as well as the rural, landscape. Once they arrived in a town, they would try to attract their audience and, following a well established practice in show business, would distribute printed sheets with details of the performance to come.

This sheet, which has been dated around 1770, is a good example of this sort of printed matter, though it has proved impossible to find out anything about the small group of itinerants whose show it announced. Neither can we say in what towns it was performed. But we know that the main attraction of their performance was a large double microscope

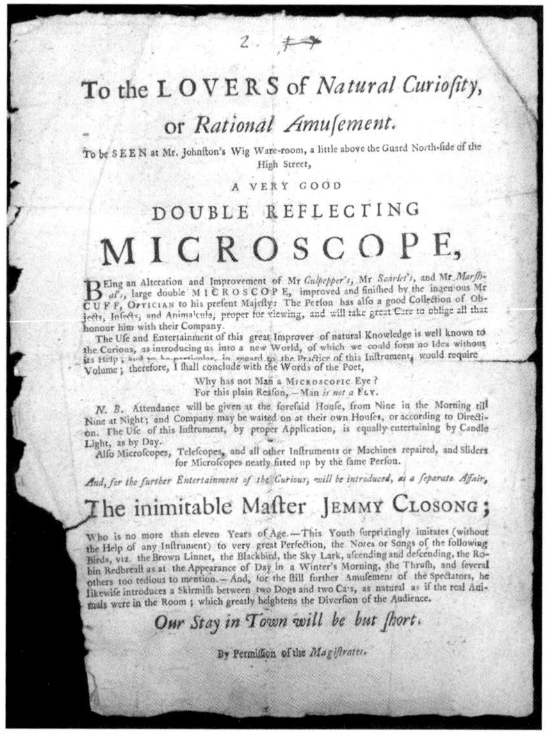

2.

To the LOVERS of *Natural Curioſity*,
or *Rational Amuſement*.

To be SEEN at Mr. Johnſton's Wig Ware-room, a little above the Guard North-ſide of the High Street,

A VERY GOOD

DOUBLE REFLECTING

MICROSCOPE,

BEing an Alteration and Improvement of Mr *Culpepper's*, Mr *Scarlet's*, and Mr *Marſhal's*, large double MICROSCOPE, improved and finiſhed by the ingenious Mr CUFF, OPTICIAN to his preſent Majeſty: The Perſon has alſo a good Collection of Objects, Inſects, and Animalcula, proper for viewing, and will take great Care to oblige all that honour him with their Company.

The Uſe and Entertainment of this great Improver of natural Knowledge is well known to the Curious, as introducing us into a new World, of which we could form no Idea without its Help; and to be particular, in regard to the Practice of this Inſtrument, would require Volume; therefore, I ſhall conclude with the Words of the Poet,

Why has not Man a MICROSCOPIC Eye?
For this plain Reaſon,—Man *is not a* FLY.

N. B. Attendance will be given at the foreſaid Houſe, from Nine in the Morning till Nine at Night; and Company may be waited on at their own Houſes, or according to Direction. The Uſe of this Inſtrument, by proper Application, is equally entertaining by Candle Light, as by Day.

Alſo Microſcopes, Teleſcopes, and all other Inſtruments or Machines repaired, and Sliders for Microſcopes neatly fitted up by the ſame Perſon.

And, for the further Entertainment of the Curious, will be introduced, as a ſeparate Affair,

The inimitable Maſter JEMMY CLOSONG;

Who is no more than eleven Years of Age.—This Youth ſurprizingly imitates (without the Help of any Inſtrument) to very great Perfection, the Notes or Songs of the following Birds, viz. the Brown Linnet, the Blackbird, the Sky Lark, aſcending and deſcending, the Robin Redbreaſt as at the Appearance of Day in a Winter's Morning, the Thruſh, and ſeveral others too tedious to mention.—And, for the ſtill further Amuſement of the Spectators, he likewiſe introduces a Skirmiſh between two Dogs and two Cats, as natural as if the real Animals were in the Room; which greatly heightens the Diverſion of the Audience.

Our Stay in Town will be but ſhort.

By Permiſſion of the *Magiſtrates*.

Advertisement of a microscope show in eighteenth-century England. Catalogue no. 45.

of the type made by the London maker John Cuff, and a collection of objects to be seen through it. Although the person organising the event could not claim to be an instrument maker, he did advertise his skills in repairing optical instruments. His performance with the microscope was complemented by that of a young boy particularly gifted in imitating birds' songs and other animal noises. Together they had struck a deal with a certain Mr Johnston, who allowed them to use his wig warehouse as a stage. The show could also be put on at the house of a spectator or in any other venue. Lovers of natural curiosity and rational entertainment were the main target of the advertisement; to these wonder-mongers, a microscope and a boy imitating birds, dogs and cats were part of the same kind of amusement which nature, aptly manipulated by man, could offer.

Schaffer (1993).

46. George Adams (1709–1772)

A treatise describing the construction, and explaining the use of new celestial and terrestrial globes. Designed to illustrate, in the most easy and natural manner, the phoenomena of the earth and heavens, and to shew the correspondence of the two spheres. With a great variety of astronomical and geographical problems. By George Adams. The fourth edition.

London, printed for and sold by the author, 1777
8°; [a]8 b6 B-Z8 2A4

George Adams embodied the success and recognition to which a London instrument maker could aspire in the eighteenth century. Well known among the virtuosi and the aristocracy, he enjoyed the King's patronage and in 1760 became Mathematical Instrument Maker to George III. He supplied the instruments for the 1769 voyage of Captain Cook. He complemented his

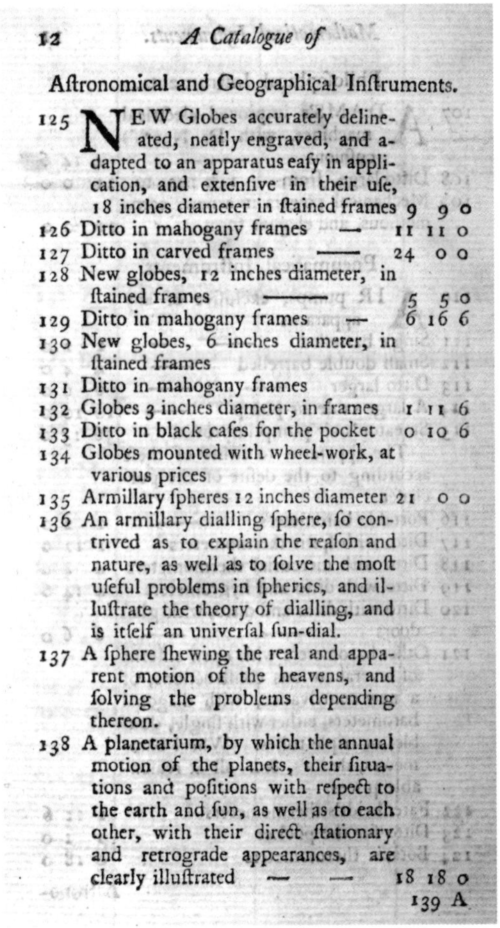
12 *A Catalogue of*

Aftronomical and Geographical Inftruments.

125	NEW Globes accurately delineated, neatly engraved, and adapted to an apparatus eafy in application, and extenfive in their ufe, 18 inches diameter in ftained frames	9	9	0
126	Ditto in mahogany frames —	11	11	0
127	Ditto in carved frames ——	24	0	0
128	New globes, 12 inches diameter, in ftained frames ——	5	5	0
129	Ditto in mahogany frames —	6	16	6
130	New globes, 6 inches diameter, in ftained frames			
131	Ditto in mahogany frames			
132	Globes 3 inches diameter, in frames	1	11	6
133	Ditto in black cafes for the pocket	0	10	6
134	Globes mounted with wheel-work, at various prices			
135	Armillary fpheres 12 inches diameter	21	0	0
136	An armillary dialling fphere, fo contrived as to explain the reafon and nature, as well as to folve the moft ufeful problems in fpherics, and illuftrate the theory of dialling, and is itfelf an univerfal fun-dial.			
137	A fphere fhewing the real and apparent motion of the heavens, and folving the problems depending thereon.			
138	A planetarium, by which the annual motion of the planets, their fituations and pofitions with refpect to the earth and fun, as well as to each other, with their direct ftationary and retrograde appearances, are clearly illuftrated — —	18	18	0

139 A

Instruments for every pocket: a page from the catalogue of George Adams.
Catalogue no. 46.

activities as an instrument maker with the publication of books. One of these was his popular treatise on the use of globes. First published in 1766, it went through four subsequent editions in less than twenty years. Adams showed a flair for business and took full advantage of the increasing popularity of natural investigations among various social strata. For example, in the catalogue of his instruments appended to the fourth edition of his *Treatise*, he addressed 'Gentlemen, Ladies, Merchants etc.', and stressed that even people with the meanest faculties could enjoy mathematics and experimental philosophy.

Adams' first published catalogue of mathematical, philosophical and optical instruments appeared in his *Micrographia* in 1746 with no prices; in later versions prices were included. Adams revised his catalogue and regularly added it to his publications, even if surviving copies show that it was also meant to circulate separately.

The catalogue was organised under various headings, and included instruments as varied as drawing pens, pedometers for surveyors, reflecting telescopes and amazingly expensive orreries. Three features stand out. First, the emphasis Adams put on the fact that he would himself inspect the making of the instruments and that all the pieces would be assembled in his house. Parts of the instruments were obviously produced by different makers and subsequently put together in Adams' workshop: it was important to reassure customers that Adams would inspect each object. Second, Adams' statement that instruments could be applied to several operations so that they 'may not be multiplied without necessity' was complemented by the opposite practice of producing a range of cheaper or dearer instruments of the same kind, so as to meet the purchasing powers of different categories of customers: the multiplication of his stock was part of Adams' success. Third, the presence of numbers corresponding to each instrument was meant to help customers with their orders: theoretically, they could just refer to the numbers. But compared to later catalogues, it is surprising to discover how meagre the description of some of these instruments was: for example there is no explanation why one version of Hadley's quadrant costs two pounds and another four.

King and Millburn (1978); Anderson, Burnett and Gee (1990); Bryden (1992); Walters (1992); Morton and Wess (1993); Millburn (2000).

47. Benjamin Pike (1809–1864)

Pike's illustrated descriptive catalogue of optical, mathematical, and philosophical instruments, manufactured, imported, and sold by the author; with the prices affixed at which they are offered in 1848. With upwards of 750 engravings. By Benjamin Pike, Jr. In two volumes.

New York, published and sold by the author, 1848
2 volumes

Benjamin Pike, Jr., the son of an instrument maker, opened his shop in New York in 1843. Instrument making was still little developed in the States, although things changed after 1848, when German opticians emigrating after the upheavals in their country imported expertise and new business. Pike was keen on innovations and produced a wide range of instruments, including surveying, pneumatic and electrical apparatus. He won several awards.

Pike's catalogue of 1848 was much broader than any published previously in the US and included detailed descriptions and technical explanations which made it more a textbook than a sale list. Such abundance of detail and clear illustrations were meant to meet the needs of customers living outside New York, who would use the catalogue to choose and order their instruments. Most were school-teachers of science working in remote areas, at whom Pike aimed variously priced sets of apparatus for specific sciences. He also mentioned parents and 'guardians of youth' who were encouraged to buy apparatus which would greatly and usefully entertain their children.

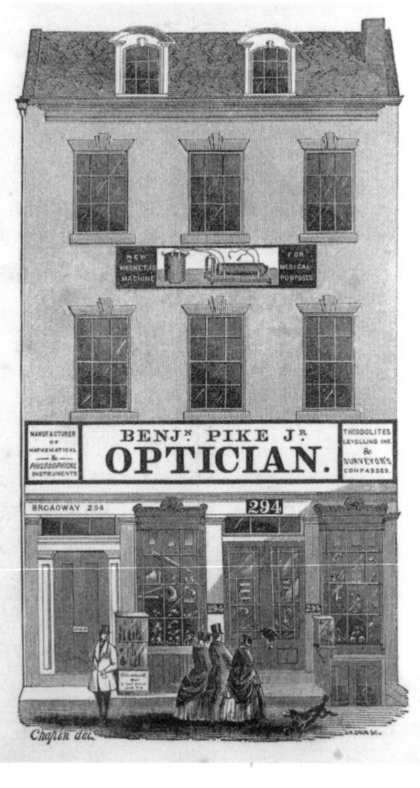

The shop of the instrument maker Benjamin Pike in nineteenth-century New York. Catalogue no. 47.

Pike boasted of his recent magnetical machines for medical purposes. Although to preserve patients' privacy he refused to add descriptions of the cases in which such apparatus had been effective, he stressed that hospitals and private citizens, both local and foreign, had bought them. A final list of all the instruments on offer, together with their prices, concludes this catalogue of more than five hundred pages. Elite American scientists would probably have turned to European makers to equip their laboratories; but by counting on the growing role of science teaching, by offering a surprisingly broad range of instruments, some of which he imported from Paris and London, and by shrewdly taking advantage of sale by catalogue, Pike succeeded in establishing a very prosperous business. The catalogue went into a second edition in 1856.

Brenni (1989); Warner (1993).

48. Cambridge Scientific Instrument Company. Various sale-catalogues and postcards (1920–1950)

In the decade after World War I British scientific instrument companies were in dire straits. Having lost the War Ministry's orders, the two potential customers were manufacturers increasingly requiring instruments for monitoring the production process, and the research market of both university and industrial sectors. The management of the Cambridge Scientific Instrument Company, later the Cambridge Instrument Company (CIC), of which Whipple was a prominent figure, was successful in cultivating both clients. The company also turned to the stronger American market and struck deals with overseas firms. Although British instrument-making companies have been considered slow to develop marketing strategies and publicity, the CIC was keen to improve its advertising policy.

Trade catalogues, for example, which had been published regularly since the early days, were diversified. The functional, but grey catalogues embodied in *Physiological instruments* of 1899 were replaced by fancier publications such as *Radiation and optical pyrometers* (1927) in red covers with a multicoloured image, and the even brighter *Cambridge instruments for food and drink industries* (1932). They show the effort CIC put into packaging technical information in an appealing form. But we should not take catalogues at face value. They might even advertise goods which the firm was not yet able to produce. Whipple himself admitted to compiling a catalogue which included instruments the company should, but did not yet, make.

To diversify trade literature further, the CIC published the 'handy six': six booklets of the unusual size of 11 by 14 cm, marketed as reference works on popular instruments. In the 1950s the CIC started a series of publications including historical and biographical information on the men who had designed instruments or contributed to their improvement. History was here transformed into an advertising medium.

Advertising accuracy: a postcard of the Cambridge Instrument Company
Catalogue no. 48.

Since the mid-nineteenth century, a popular advertising strategy was to contact prospective customers by mail: postcards were the latest development of this fashion. The management of the CIC was quick to exploit this technique and a wide range of postcards advertising both the instruments and the literature that accompanied them became part of the public image of the company.

Whipple (1942); Scarlett (1978); Nevett (1982); Anderson, Burnett and Gee (1990); Williams (1994).

49. The Scientific Instrument Manufacturers' Association of Great Britain

Handbook

[London], 1943
53 p.

As a result of rising membership and diversifying interest, in 1935 the British Optical Instrument Manufacturers' Association changed its name to the Scientific Instrument Manufacturers' Association of Great Britain. It had three main aims: to protect the interests of the members, for example by establishing links with the Government, to support research and to finance education of the workforce.

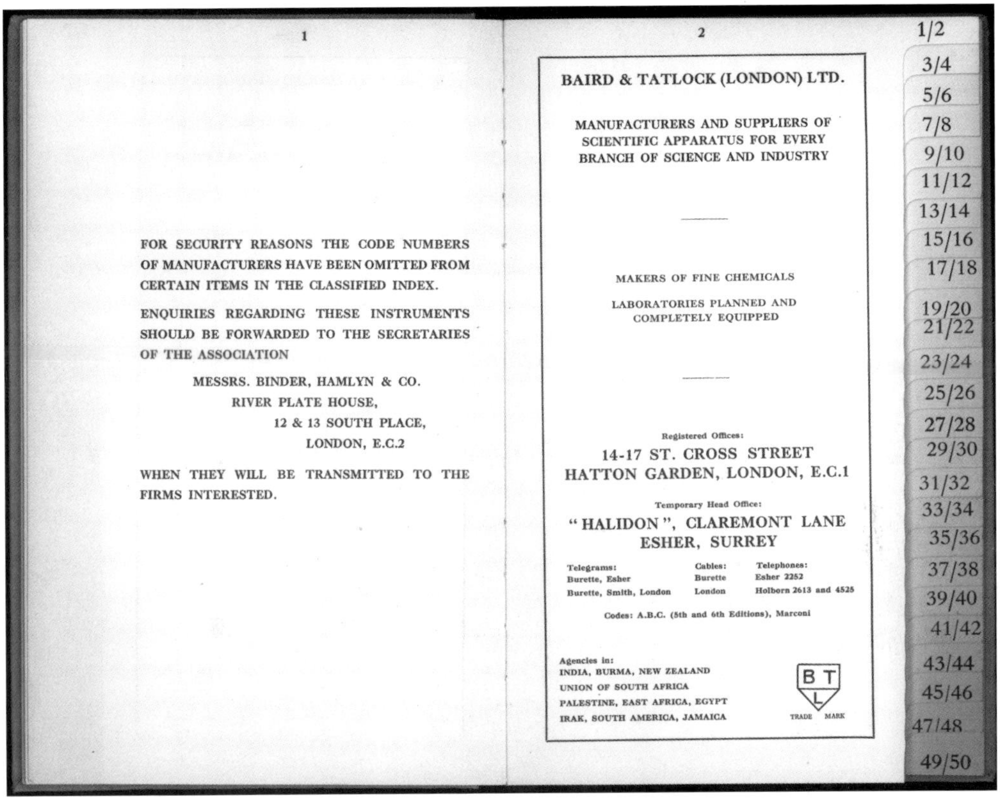

1

FOR SECURITY REASONS THE CODE NUMBERS OF MANUFACTURERS HAVE BEEN OMITTED FROM CERTAIN ITEMS IN THE CLASSIFIED INDEX.

ENQUIRIES REGARDING THESE INSTRUMENTS SHOULD BE FORWARDED TO THE SECRETARIES OF THE ASSOCIATION

MESSRS. BINDER, HAMLYN & CO.
RIVER PLATE HOUSE,
12 & 13 SOUTH PLACE,
LONDON, E.C.2

WHEN THEY WILL BE TRANSMITTED TO THE FIRMS INTERESTED.

2

BAIRD & TATLOCK (LONDON) LTD.

MANUFACTURERS AND SUPPLIERS OF SCIENTIFIC APPARATUS FOR EVERY BRANCH OF SCIENCE AND INDUSTRY

MAKERS OF FINE CHEMICALS

LABORATORIES PLANNED AND COMPLETELY EQUIPPED

Registered Offices:
14-17 ST. CROSS STREET
HATTON GARDEN, LONDON, E.C.1

Temporary Head Office:
" HALIDON ", CLAREMONT LANE
ESHER, SURREY

Telegrams:	Cables:	Telephones:
Burette, Esher	Burette	Esher 2252
Burette, Smith, London	London	Holborn 2613 and 4525

Codes: A.B.C. (5th and 6th Editions), Marconi

Agencies in:
INDIA, BURMA, NEW ZEALAND
UNION OF SOUTH AFRICA
PALESTINE, EAST AFRICA, EGYPT
IRAK, SOUTH AMERICA, JAMAICA

Keeping knowledge confidential: limited information about scientific instrument manufacture in the directory of the SIMA.
Catalogue no. 49.

This handbook was published in September 1943 with the aim of providing members with an up-to-date directory. It included a list of officers, the regulations of the association, and a brief historical essay by Robert Whipple. But the bulk of the book, organised with a thumb index, comprised information about the companies. Each had a page to supply details of their production and their addresses. An index of products opened the publication. Yet this was not a proper publication, as a note at the foot of the title-page clearly states: 'Private and confidential, not to be published'. Furthermore, a number of instruments had been omitted from the index for security reasons. As Whipple wrote in his introduction celebrating the success of the British industry: 'instruments are the eyes and ears of ships and aircraft and the nerve centres of armies and navies in attack and defence'. No wonder that, especially in wartime, the purpose of providing information about the instrument trade should be counterbalanced by concerns about secrecy. On the one hand scientific companies had fully embraced the rhetoric of the openness of science; on the other, nobody knew better the advantages of keeping knowledge confidential.

Williams (1994).

4

Making a Collector

The first three sections of this catalogue explored various aspects of the production and use of books on instruments, chosen from those collected by Whipple. This final section takes a reflexive turn and focuses on the books which Whipple bought to help himself become a collector. It presents fourteen volumes from what we may think of as the 'reference shelf' in Whipple's library. All but one were published in the twentieth century and served Whipple as aids in his collecting and in familiarising himself with contemporary research in the history of instruments and of science. They are very heterogeneous, and include catalogues of private collections, books published to celebrate the anniversaries of scientific 'landmarks' and specialised bibliographies, but also elegant reprints of classics of science, catalogues of auctions and surveys of the history of science.

Today such volumes tend to be relegated to a library's store. But they are fundamental sources for recapturing the expectations and the day-to-day activities of a collector like Whipple, who, apart from two notebooks which he used as accession registers of his purchases, left neither a rich correspondence nor a diary. Sometimes, though, traces of how Whipple read and used these volumes remain in the books, for example, a letter with the translation of a paragraph attached to a German book on mathematical instruments, or the dense scribbling in his copy of John Fulton's bibliography of Boyle, in which he recorded the prices of his own acquisitions. We can guess at his use of the other books. The six-volume catalogue of the Conservatoire des Arts et Métiers of Paris probably served as a sort of encyclopaedia of instruments; William Dampier's *Short history of science* (1945) was informative reading, one of the few histories of science available in the 1940s which took account of the latest developments. John Louis Emil Dreyer's copy of the *Historia coelestis*, which is the only pre-1900 book in this section and includes Tycho Brahe's observations, reminded Whipple of how little care historians of astronomy took of their rare books, while the elegant translation of Gilbert's *De magnete* (1900) by Silvanus Thompson was a Victorian example of bibliophilia applied to past science.

In addition to opening a window onto how Whipple read and collected, there is a second reason for taking these books seriously. They are the products of the extremely varied community of people who in the first half of the twentieth century were active in preserving and researching the material evidence of past science, or in writing histories of science for a growing readership. Most of them are now very little known; some, for example Edward N. Da Costa Andrade and Robert Gunther, are familiar only to specialists. They had different backgrounds and approached science books and instruments of the past with different expertise: some were scientists, others dealers, others art historians. Some knew each other, others belonged to different milieux. They all worked at a time when the history of science was increasingly used to celebrate contemporary science, but was not yet the turf of academics and professional historians. Most of them were collectors or were closely linked to the world of collecting. They would regularly go to antiquarian shops, auctions, libraries and museums; sometimes they worked in them. Placed at the intersection between a growing trade in scientific 'relics'—both instruments and books—and scholarly research, they produced knowledge about past science.

In many accounts of the history of the history of science the decades between the 1930s and 1950s are represented as pivotal for future developments in the discipline. Emphasis is placed on major ideological clashes, in particular between Marxist and non-Marxist scholars, and on the ensuing historiographical conflicts. Recent work has reassessed the impact of such antagonism on the everyday practice of contemporary historians. Probably it was not until the 1950s and the Cold War that such antagonism became so dominant (Shapin 1992). More importantly, that strife has distracted historians from the fact that most research into the history of science carried out in the first half of the twentieth century was based on collecting practices and the expertise that shaped them. Despite some pioneering studies (Turner, A. 1987, 1995; Bennett 1997a), the activities of non-academic collectors, dealers, museum staff and bibliographers, whose work proved essential to later professional historians, is still hardly visible. But it was in their hands that collecting science 'relics', both privately and publicly, became a widespread phenomenon. It was obviously an integral part, and one of the results, of a long-standing politics of promoting science and its values among a wider audience. More research is needed to understand why and how possessing scientific instruments and books came to have a similar social function to owning objects of art or first editions of the classics of English literature. The establishment of major science museums, the increasing use of public displays of science, and the inclusion of scientific objects in the notion of national heritage also require further investigation. At the centre of all these processes was the lively and varied community of collectors and dealers of which Whipple was a member. Their activities were crucial in defining the categories of antique scientific instruments and rare books of science, on which so much of subsequent research depended (Bennett 1998). The books on Whipple's 'reference shelf' are a sample of their works and the tools they used.

50. *A catalogue of the collection of antique microscopes, formed by the late Sir Frank Crisp. Which will be sold at Stevens's Auction Rooms on Tuesday, February 17th, 1925.*

London, Riddle, Smith & Duffus, 1925
31 p.

The fate of Sir Frank Crisp's collection of microscopes is one of the most interesting chapters in the history of collecting scientific instruments in England. Crisp (1843–1919) was a

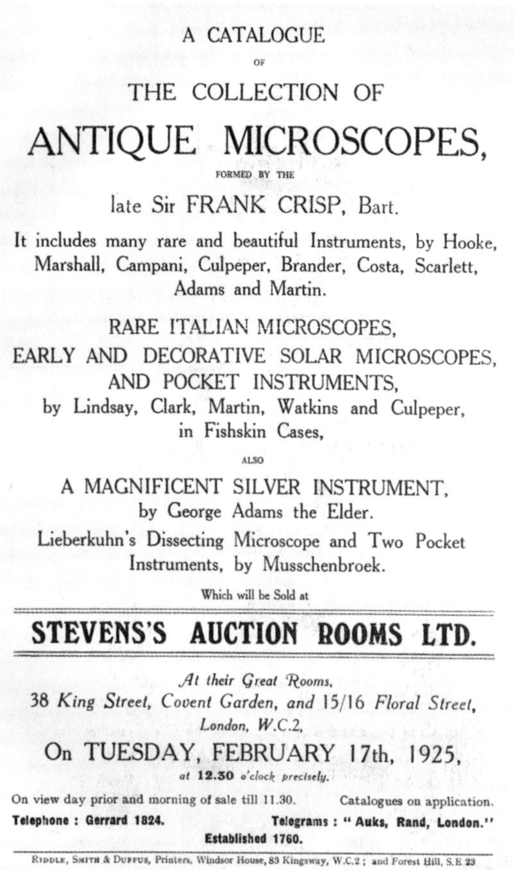

A CATALOGUE

OF

THE COLLECTION OF

ANTIQUE MICROSCOPES,

FORMED BY THE

late Sir FRANK CRISP, Bart.

It includes many rare and beautiful Instruments, by Hooke, Marshall, Campani, Culpeper, Brander, Costa, Scarlett, Adams and Martin.

RARE ITALIAN MICROSCOPES,
EARLY AND DECORATIVE SOLAR MICROSCOPES,
AND POCKET INSTRUMENTS,
by Lindsay, Clark, Martin, Watkins and Culpeper,
in Fishskin Cases,

ALSO

A MAGNIFICENT SILVER INSTRUMENT,
by George Adams the Elder.

Lieberkuhn's Dissecting Microscope and Two Pocket Instruments, by Musschenbroek.

Which will be Sold at

STEVENS'S AUCTION ROOMS LTD.

At their Great Rooms,
38 *King Street, Covent Garden, and* 15/16 *Floral Street, London, W.C.2,*

On TUESDAY, FEBRUARY 17th, 1925,

at **12.30** *o'clock precisely.*

On view day prior and morning of sale till 11.30. Catalogues on application.

Telephone : Gerrard 1824. Telegrams : "Auks, Rand, London."

Established 1760.

Riddle, Smith & Duffus, Printers, Windsor House, 83 Kingsway, W.C.2; and Forest Hill, S.E. 23

The frontispiece of the catalogue of the famous Crisp auction in 1925. Catalogue no. 50.

successful company lawyer, who cultivated his hobby of collecting microscopes on a massive scale. To carry out his purchases, he hired an agent. An active member of the Royal Microscopical Society, Crisp translated a very popular German work on optics, but his interest in microscopes remained limited to the history of the instruments and never included microscopical practice. After his death in 1919, various people and institutions quarrelled over his huge collection: the family was willing to sell it, but staff at the Science Museum in London and the Pitt Rivers Museum in Oxford were both under the impression that Crisp had made arrangements to bequeath his three thousand microscopes to them. Eventually, the collection was auctioned. The community of museum keepers and collectors perceived this as a major defeat and a serious loss. It was Robert Whipple who recalled in 1926 that it was because Crisp had made clear his intention to leave his microscopes to the Nation, that he had been allowed to remove the microscopes belonging to the George III collection from King's College London. Instead, they became part of the sensational transaction which took place in 1925 at Stevens's Auction Rooms. Private collectors, agents and museum keepers gathered at what must have been a dramatic event; Thomas H. Court (catalogue no. 51) played a major role, probably writing the descriptions in the auction catalogue and securing a number of microscopes for the Science Museum. The whole episode is an interesting example of the still fluid boundaries between the notion of private and public property at a time when the business surrounding antique scientific instruments was thriving, but they were increasingly regarded as part of the national heritage. Like many other copies of this catalogue, Whipple's copy is complemented by manuscript notes of the price of the various lots.

Later on Whipple acquired several books on microscopy which had belonged to Crisp.

Whipple (1926); Insley (1982; 1984); Turner, G. L'E. (1989b).

51. Reginald S. Clay (1869–1954) and Thomas H. Court (1868–1951)

The history of the microscope. Compiled from original instruments and documents, up to the introduction of the achromatic microscope. By Reginald S. Clay and Thomas H. Court.

London, Charles Griffin and Company, 1932
xiv, 266 p.

Of all modern scientific instruments microscopes enjoyed the greatest popularity among a broad community of amateurs. And when antique instruments started to become collectable objects, microscopes were also the easiest and most affordable items collectors could buy. In the first decades of the twentieth century, various museums of science were founded: often based on private donations, they usually held a large number of microscopes. A growing community of both private collectors and museum staff required advice and guidelines in order to make judicious acquisitions. Collectors were Clay and Court's main intended readership.

Court was one of the most active instrument dealers in London in the 1920s and 1930s, and also worked for the Science Museum. Clay was a physicist with a passion for antique instruments: his collection of microscopes was one of the largest in the country. Between them they had access to an extraordinarily wide range of microscopes. In the 1920s they published several papers on the history of microscopes and optics, mainly in the *Transactions of the optical society.* Building on that work, they published a proper monograph.

Popular books on scientific instruments usually had historical introductions, but the abundance of technical details which this volume provided was meant to help collectors identify and evaluate antique items. The book was mainly a compilation of passages on microscopes

A microscope from the collection of King George III in the historical survey by Reginald Clay and Thomas H. Court. Catalogue no. 51.

from works published over the centuries, and included biographical information on a number of instrument makers. This lack of original research has recently attracted some criticism; yet, at a time when knowledge about instruments was limited, it was thanks to this type of publication that collectors could start building their expertise. It is likely that Clay and Court as well as their readers, including Whipple, valued earlier books on science mainly as sources of information on instruments.

Heywood (1969); Insley (1982); Turner, G. L'E. (1989b).

52. Alfred Rohde-Hamburg (1892–1945)

Die Geschichte der wissenschaftlichen Instrumente vom Beginn der Renaissance bis zum Ausgang des 18. Jahrhunderts. Von Alfred Rohde-Hamburg.

Leipzig, Verlag von Klinkhardt & Biermann, 1923
viii, 119 p.

The transformation of scientific instruments into collectable objects which occurred at the end of the nineteenth century was fundamentally about their aesthetization. Collectors would look for precious materials and elaborate decoration but show little interest in the bulky apparatus which had increasingly filled up laboratories or in their role in the history of science. In the widespread fascination for applied art, for example, astrolabes, watches and sundials were collected primarily as evidence of past design and craftsmanship. A thriving trade in these objects fed the collectors and the newly established national museums of applied art. Small wonder that one of the first people to write a historical study of scientific instruments was a German art historian and museum cura-

Abb. 95. Philipp Danfery-Rouen. Auftragbussole 1658.

Abb. 96. Etienne Delaune.
David erschlägt Goliath, Stich.

Research into the source of an instrument decoration in Alfred Rohde's work.
Catalogue no. 52.

tor, Alfred Rohde. His *History of scientific instruments from the beginning of the Renaissance to the end of the eighteenth century* appeared in a series of publications devoted to the history of applied art which included another book by Rohde on eighteenth-century wrought iron work, as well as Julius von Schlosser's seminal book on Renaissance *Wunderkammern.*

Rohde studied art history and philosophy in Marburg, Munich and Paris and received his doctorate in 1916. He then worked in the museums of art and applied art in Hamburg and Königsberg. In the introduction to this volume he argued strongly for a history of instruments free from technical and mathematical details. Instruments should be studied either as examples of an artistic style or in connection with an important personality, such as Brahe or Galilei, so that they would become an element in a broader history of culture and art. That instruments were useful tools in mathematical and astronomical research should be considered an integral part of their artistic charm. The catalogues of Frédéric Spitzer's collection and of the Roussel collection were examples of the approach which Rohde promoted.

While it is difficult to say what Whipple made of this point of view, we know that he was interested in how Rohde discussed astrolabes. Since Whipple could not read German, he asked a friend to help him with a translation of the relevant pages and kept that friend's letter in the book.

Turner, A. (1987; 1995); Killy and Vierhaus (1998).

53. Henri Michel (1885–1981)

Introduction a l'étude d'une collection d'instruments anciens de mathématiques.

Anvers, De Sikkel, 1939
105, [6] p.

A Belgian engineer combining expertise in the history of astronomy with a deep interest in art history and music, Henri Michel devoted much of his time to collecting and studying antique astronomical instruments and developed an acute awareness of their problematic nature. He wrote dozens of publications and was active in various societies such as the Centre National Belge d'Histoire des Sciences and the Société International de l'Astrolabe.

In his *Introduction to the study of a collection of antique mathematical instruments,* Michel presented a few items from the collection he had assembled over twenty years. The basis of his fascination for mathematical instruments was their combination of elegant design and efficient function. Here Michel was openly drawing on one of the principles promoted by contemporary art theory, that beauty lies in simplicity and functionality. However, instruments were a category of objects which still lacked adequate criteria of classification. For

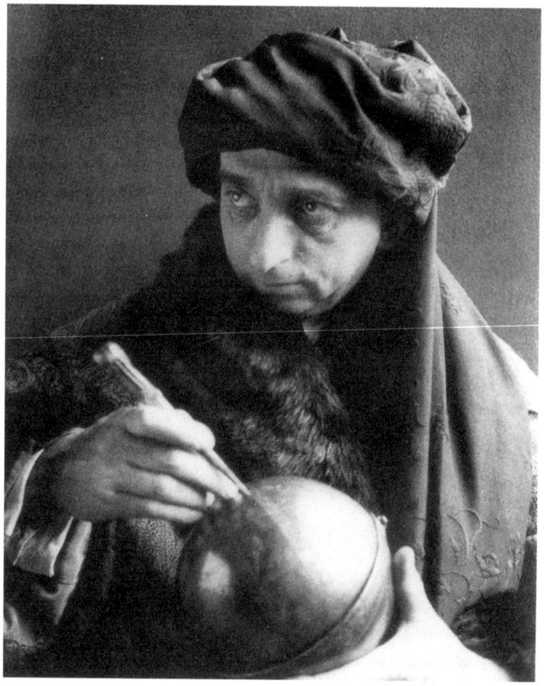

Portrait of a collector: Henri Michel dressed up as an Arab and holding a sphere.
Catalogue no. 53.

example, to group instruments according to their apparent use was satisfactory in the framework of a history of technology, but introduced artificial distinctions among objects which, like astrolabes, were often employed in different fields. Moreover, Michel argued, such 'cold' distinctions were one of the reasons why very few people visited science museums. He favoured a chronological classification, which would allow scholars to place instruments at once within the history of crafts, art history and the history of science, to all of which they belonged.

A collector and connoisseur, Michel opposed some features of academia, including a style of writing loaded with footnotes and references. As an alternative, in the last chapter of this volume he offered an example of more creative writing, and reported an imaginary conversation between various savants in a French salon at the end of the eighteenth century. In the same polemical vein, Michel chose to appear in this volume exotically wearing a turban and holding a sphere. Nothing could be more different from Whipple's self-fashioning, but the two men were friends. In 1947 Michel presented Whipple with a copy of his book; the dedication reads: 'May this introduction be a recollection of his own collection'.

Hoge (1982); De Graeve (1982).

54. Robert T. Gunther (1869–1940)

Early science in Oxford. By R. T. Gunther.

Oxford, printed for the subscribers, 1922–45
14 volumes

In the 1910s Robert Gunther embarked on mapping scientific instruments and books held in Oxford colleges. It was the first step in what would become a life-long project of an archaeology of science, that is, research into all the material evidence of natural investigations pursued in Oxford over the centuries. For biographical and historical reasons, this

Mechanical models at Oriel College, Oxford.
Catalogue no. 54.

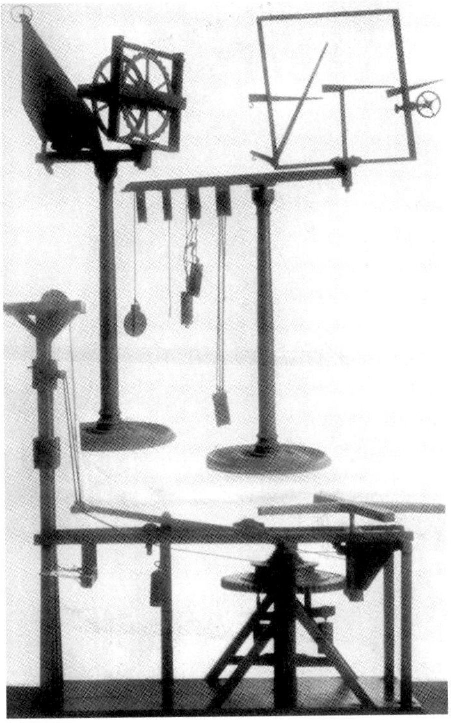

project stirred up controversies, but it is representative of an 'antiquarian' interest in scientific instruments which shaped the activities of a number of collectors and curators. Gunther was a model for many of them, including Whipple, whose decision to bequeath his collection of books and instruments to the University of Cambridge was certainly influenced by his friend in Oxford.

In the early 1920s, following the donation of Lewis Evans' collection of sundials to the University, Gunther persistently tried to convince the University that the Old Ashmolean Museum should be converted into a proper museum of the history of science. It was only in 1935 and after many discussions that the museum opened. As part of this commitment to the cause of scientific objects, Gunther embarked on a substantial publishing project which included both results of his research and the reprints of some classics in the history of British science. Among the former were a remarkable catalogue of astrolabes of the world, and the fourteen volumes of *Early science in Oxford*, a 'stock-taking of the scientific resources of the University of Oxford', as Gunther put it. The result was a mixed series of volumes, consisting of detailed lists of antique instruments possessed by Oxford colleges, collections of unpublished documents, and biographies of important Oxford scientists, for example Robert Hooke.

Unlike Alfred Rohde and Henri Michel (catalogue nos. 52 and 53), Gunther was driven by an interest in instruments as sources for investigating the progress of science. He studied them in relation to relevant scientific literature and his work was fundamental in establishing criteria of classification. Consideration of the instruments' artistic value remained marginal. Arguing that Oxford had a special place in the history of early modern science, he regarded his project as locally based and at the same time internationally relevant. But probably due to wider misunderstandings between Gunther and the academic establishment, he failed to convince Oxford University Press fully to embark on the project: the fourteen volumes were published by subscription, and advertisement and distribution remained entirely in the author's hands.

Gunther, A. E. (1967); Simcock (1985); Turner, A. (1987); Bennett (1994; 1997).

55. Ministère du Commerce, de l'Industrie, des Postes et des Télégraphes.

Catalogue officiel des collections du Conservatoire National des Arts et Métiers.

Paris, E. Bernard, 1905–1910
6 volumes

The production of a satisfactory taxonomy of scientific instruments was a complicated process which became increasingly urgent as public museums of science and technology opened at the end of the nineteenth century. While celebrating national achievements, they often had pedagogical functions. Expertise in the sometimes unusual items on display became sought-after, while printed catalogues were the essential outcome of this new process of documentation. One of the most interesting museums where collecting, cataloguing and displaying instruments took place in the nineteenth century was the venerable Conservatoire National des Arts et Métiers in Paris.

Founded in 1794 and opened in 1800, the Conservatoire was meant to bring together collections of agricultural and industrial machinery while providing technical education and encouragement for economic improvement. In 1818, after new major acquisitions, the first catalogue of the collection was published. It was organised topographically; in comparison to the agricultural and industrial collections, scientific instruments were scarce. Under the directorship of the physicist Arthur Morin, who had won the support of Napoleon III, the Conservatoire became the repository of up-to-date technology, as well as a historical museum. In 1851, Morin edited a new catalogue. It ran to various revised editions during the century, until in 1905 the official catalogue of the collections started to be published. In six volumes, this was not a coffee-table book, but a working tool. Thousands of objects were listed and very briefly described according to the various sciences and crafts to which they belonged. By bringing together a huge variety of objects which embodied every aspect of science and technology, these catalogues made it clear how challenging the project of preserving the materials of science was, especially when instruments and tools were regarded as sources for historical research and not just of aesthetic pleasure.

Turner, A. (1987); Mercier (1994); Jacomi (1995).

A silk mathematical model at the Conservatoire National des Arts et Métiers in Paris.
Catalogue no. 55.

56. Heinrich Zeitlinger (1871–1960) and Henry C. Sotheran (1861–1928)

Bibliotheca chemico-mathematica. Catalogue of works in many tongues on exact and applied science, with a subject-index. Compiled and annotated by H. Z. and H. C. S.

London, Henry Sotheran and Co., 1921–1952
6 volumes

Henry Sotheran was one of the first London antique dealers fully to appreciate the potential of books of science. After taking over his father's established business in 1893, he employed the Austrian born Heinrich Zeitlinger, whose work and erudition greatly contributed to shaping the firm's specific interest in scientific books. Zeitlinger was responsible for the production of printed catalogues; after the death of Sotheran in 1928, he became director of the firm and continued to cultivate its scientific specialisation. In the competitive antiquarian book market, printed catalogues were fundamental tools to advertise the goods and establish the credentials of the business. In 1921 the first two volumes of the *Bibliotheca chemico-mathematica* came out. They included records of books on 'mathematics, astronomy, physics, and chemistry, and allied subjects' and followed an alphabetical order. Often a brief comment about the contents of the book complemented bibliographical information. The abundant illustrations allowed readers to appreciate the richness of engravings, woodcuts and other iconographical apparatus to be found in science books. The two volumes were soon followed by a series of supplements, the last of which was published in 1952. The set became an essential tool for collectors.

At a time when scientific books had just started to be considered collectable items, Zeitlinger's detailed and reliable catalogues greatly contributed to the second lives of many old volumes. Among Sotheran's major sources of books were private libraries of collectors: often they would be listed in separate catalogues. But Zeitlinger also prepared catalogues on specific subjects, such as the *Bibliotheca Viatica*, including books on roads and transport. While responding to an increasingly diversified community of book

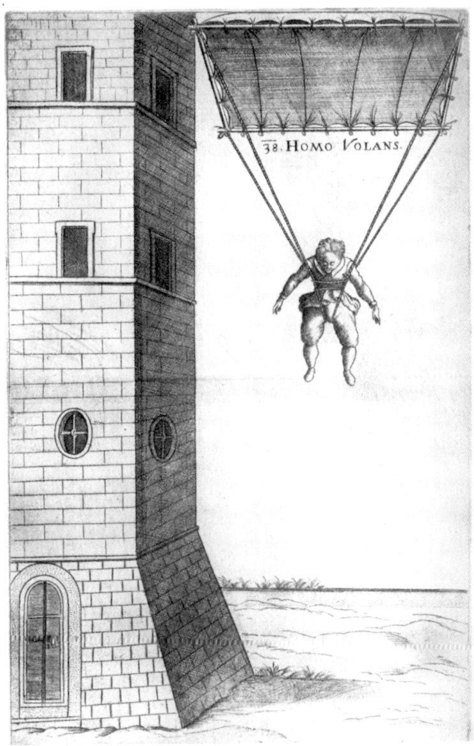

The first illustration of a parachute in an 'excessively rare' sixteenth-century book on offer at Sotheran's. Catalogue no. 56.

collectors, these catalogues also contributed to spreading the new fashion. Zeitlinger's knowledge, the thoroughness of his entries, and the final remarkably detailed subject-index made the *Bibliotheca* a reference work also for a wider public of historians and scholars.

Simmons and Chidley (1982).

57. Albert Curtz (1600–1671)

Historia coelestis. Edita complectens observationes astronomicas varias ad historiam coelestem spectantes.

Prostat apud Johannem Conradum Emmrich, 1672 [Augustae Vindelicorum Apud Simonem Utzschneiderum, 1666]
2°; 6 unsigned leaves *-15*4 16*4+1 A-2Z4 3A-3Y4 [3Z]6 4A-4Z4 5A-5Z4 6A-6H4

In 1928, Whipple bought at Sotheran's a copy of this seventeenth-century astronomical book including previously unpublished observations by Tycho Brahe. He was obviously keen on the contents of the book, but the list of previous owners appearing on the fly-leaf must have struck a special chord. Buying this copy, Whipple was confronted with evidence of a type of collecting and use of an antique book which was very different from his, and certainly fascinating.

In the nineteenth century this copy came into the hands of a series of well-known astronomers who shared an interest in Brahe. The first of these was Heinrich Christian Schumacher (1780–1850), a German astronomer who worked mostly in Denmark and published some of Brahe's observations of the comets. The book was then acquired by the Dane Hans Carl Frederik Christian Schjellerup (1827–1887), who was employed at the observatory in Copenhagen and published important star catalogues. He also did research in the history of astronomy and used Brahe's observations to derive the orbit of the comet of 1580. Schjellerup was the teacher of Johann Louis Emil Dreyer (1852–1926), a brilliant astronomer and one of the most important twentieth-century historians of astronomy. It is possible that Schjellerup gave Dreyer

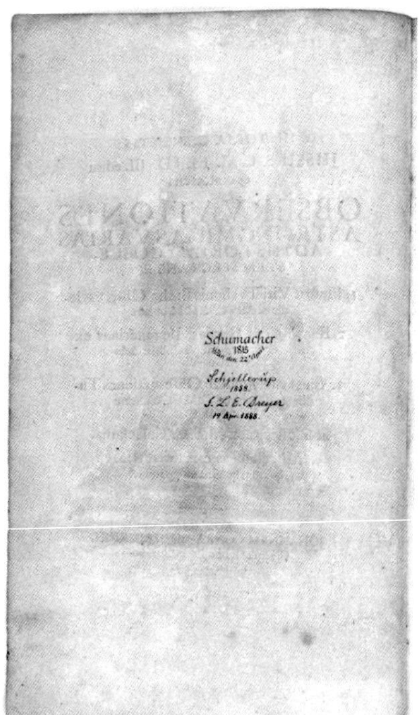

Marks of ownership in Curtz's edition of Tycho Brahe's astronomical observations.
Catalogue no. 57.

his copy of *Historia coelestis* as a token of appreciation. In 1890 Dreyer published a biography of Brahe and then started to work on the complete edition of Brahe's works and correspondence. Dreyer thought that Curtz's *Historia coelestis* was very inaccurate and that, if astronomers wanted to use Brahe's observations, a new edition was necessary. In Dreyer's hands, the copy of the *Historia coelestis* became a working tool rather than a relic of past science to be preserved. While comparing the original manuscripts of Brahe and his copy of the *Historia coelestis*, Dreyer showed no particular respect for the age of the book. He literally covered the text with what he found in the original manuscripts either in the form of small notes tipped in or as annotations written in various inks.

The result of this painstaking work appeared in volumes 10–13 of Brahe's *Opera Omnia*, published by Dreyer between 1913 and 1929 and still the definitive edition of Brahe's works. Dreyer probably thought that once his edition was available to scholars, astronomers would not find Curtz's edition of any further use and interest.

DNB; Dreyer (1963); Alexander (1981); Farrell (1981); Nielsen (1981).

58. John Farquhar Fulton (1899–1960)

A bibliography of the Honourable Robert Boyle, Fellow of the Royal Society. By J. F. Fulton.

Oxford, printed for the Society at the Oxford University Press, 1932
171 p.

Following the success of the Bibliographical Society, which was founded in London in 1892 with the aim of recovering and carefully comparing all the editions of early printed English books, in 1922 the Oxford Bibliographical Society was established. Among the first publications which the Society sponsored was John Fulton's bibliography of Boyle.

After graduating from Harvard in 1921, Fulton spent some years in Oxford, where he was admitted to the inner circle of Lady Osler, the widow of the great American physician and book collector William. On his return to the States in 1925, Fulton became a renowned physiologist and continued to collect books, assembling what would become one of the largest private medical libraries. High-ranking doctors cultivated book collecting to preserve the genteel and humanistic traits traditionally associated with medical knowledge. Collectors also contributed to the activities of bibliographical societies, for example by producing comprehensive bibliographies devoted to a specific subject or author and often based on their own possessions. In his bibliography of Boyle, Fulton was following the ground-breaking work of surgeon and fellow book collector Geoffrey Keynes, who had already published bibliographies of Thomas Browne (1924) and William Harvey (1928). Researching the editions of all Boyle's works proved a daunting job. Two volumes of *addenda* followed the first instalment of Fulton's bibliography.

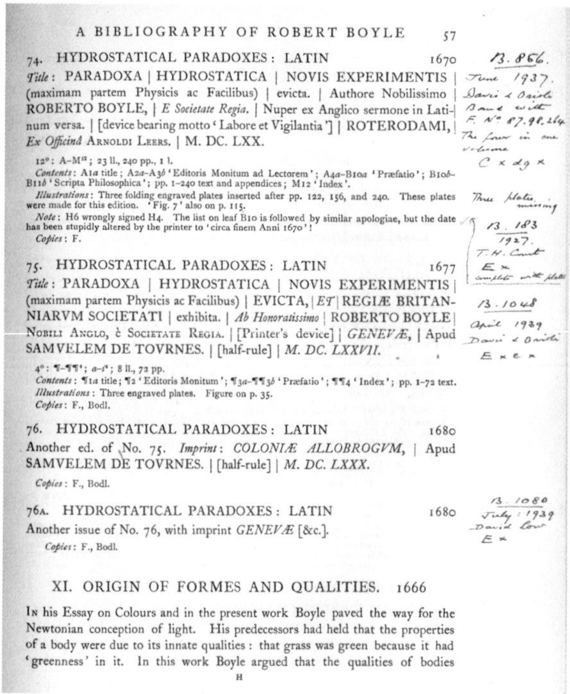

A BIBLIOGRAPHY OF ROBERT BOYLE 57

74. HYDROSTATICAL PARADOXES: LATIN 1670

Title: PARADOXA | HYDROSTATICA | NOVIS EXPERIMENTIS | (maximam partem Physicis ac Facilibus) | evicta. | Authore Nobilissimo | ROBERTO BOYLE, | *E Societate Regia.* | Nuper ex Anglico sermone in Latinum versa. | [device bearing motto 'Labore et Vigilantia'] | ROTERODAMI, | *Ex Officinâ* ARNOLDI LEERS. | M. DC. LXX.

12°: A–M¹²; 23 ll., 240 pp., 1 l.

Contents: A1*a* title; A2*a*–A3*b* 'Editoris Monitum ad Lectorem'; A4*a*–B10*a* 'Præfatio'; B10*b*–B11*b* 'Scripta Philosophica'; pp. 1–240 text and appendices; M12 'Index'.

Illustrations: Three folding engraved plates inserted after pp. 122, 156, and 240. These plates were made for this edition. 'Fig. 7' also on p. 115.

Note: H6 wrongly signed H4. The list on leaf B10 is followed by similar apologiae, but the date has been stupidly altered by the printer to 'circa finem Anni 1670'!

Copies: F.

75. HYDROSTATICAL PARADOXES: LATIN 1677

Title: PARADOXA | HYDROSTATICA | NOVIS EXPERIMENTIS | (maximam partem Physicis ac Facilibus) | EVICTA, | *ET* | REGIÆ BRITANNIARVM SOCIETATI | exhibita. | *Ab Honoratissimo* | ROBERTO BOYLE | NOBILI ANGLO, è SOCIETATE REGIA. | [Printer's device] | *GENEVÆ*, | Apud SAMVELEM DE TOVRNES. | [half-rule] | *M. DC. LXXVII.*

4°: ¶–¶¶⁴; *a*–*i*⁴; 8 ll., 72 pp.

Contents: ¶1*a* title; ¶2 'Editoris Monitum'; ¶3*a*–¶¶3*b* 'Præfatio'; ¶¶4 'Index'; pp. 1–72 text.

Illustrations: Three engraved plates. Figure on p. 35.

Copies: F., Bodl.

76. HYDROSTATICAL PARADOXES: LATIN 1680

Another ed. of No. 75. *Imprint*: *COLONIÆ ALLOBROGVM*, | Apud SAMVELEM DE TOVRNES. | [half-rule] | *M. DC. LXXX.*

Copies: F., Bodl.

76A. HYDROSTATICAL PARADOXES: LATIN 1680

Another issue of No. 76, with imprint *GENEVÆ* [&c.].

Copies: F., Bodl.

XI. ORIGIN OF FORMES AND QUALITIES. 1666

IN his Essay on Colours and in the present work Boyle paved the way for the Newtonian conception of light. His predecessors had held that the properties of a body were due to its innate qualities: that grass was green because it had 'greenness' in it. In this work Boyle argued that the qualities of bodies

H

Annotated page from John Fulton's bibliography of Boyle with the prices paid by Whipple written in an alphabetical code. Catalogue no. 58.

Fulton made his bibliographical expertise the basis for broader historical investigation. Painstaking attention to bibliographical details could provide access to Boyle's achievements. A staunch advocate of 'humanism in an age of science', Fulton was appointed Sterling Professor of History of Medicine at Yale in 1951 and became a very active member of the History of Science Society.

Boyle's books are one the major strengths of Whipple's collection. The abundant annotations on Whipple's copy of Fulton, including encoded prices, are evidence of his extensive use of the bibliography as a purchasing guide. As the creator of one of the most important philosophical instruments in the early modern period—the air-pump—and as an established icon of modern science, Boyle fitted easily into Whipple's interest in the history of instruments. Fulton's bibliography provided Whipple with a useful tool while giving his fascination for Boyle the stamp of approval of the highest and most exclusive circles of book collectors.

Le Fanu (1962); Muirhead (1962); Gariepy (1999).

59. William Gilbert (1544–1603)

William Gilbert of Colchester, physician of London. On the magnet, magnetick bodies also, and on the great magnet the earth; a new physiology, demonstrated by many arguments & experiments.

London, imprinted at the Chiswick Press, 1900
246, iv, 67 p.

This elegantly printed edition of Gilbert's famous work represents yet another way in which research in the history of science was carried out at the beginning of the twentieth century: celebration of an established icon was here combined with bibliophilia.

Frontispiece of Silvanus Thompson's commentary on Gilbert's *De magnete*. Catalogue no. 59.

Silvanus Thompson (1851–1916) was the Principal and Professor of Physics at Finsbury Technical College in London and an active member of the Institution of Electrical Engineering. He was also a knowledgeable antiquarian and possessed a substantial collection of manuscripts and books of science.

Scientists interested in the application of electricity and magnetism had a particular reverence for Gilbert, whom they perceived as a founding father. In 1889 ten members of the Institution, including Thompson, founded the Gilbert Club with the sole aim of publishing an English translation of Gilbert's Latin text. The volume was to be as close as possible to the original, except of course for the language. In 1893 a translation by Fleury Mottelay appeared in print, but to celebrate the tercentenary of the first edition in 1900, the Club was keen to produce an altogether different publication, as luxurious as it was accurate. To achieve this a deal was struck with the Chiswick Press. Since the 1840s this publisher had built up an excellent reputation by providing elegant book design and fine press work which was lacking in the output of larger printing houses working for the mass market. In particular, thanks to a unique stock of types, ornaments and initials based on models found in fifteenth- and sixteenth-century books, the Chiswick Press specialised in historical reprints. Thompson was a great admirer of the Chiswick Press and employed it for many other works.

The translation of Gilbert's *De magnete* was carried out by members of the Club, but Thompson revised the whole work and added a detailed commentary, the outcome of his years of research on Gilbert. His accurate commentary was bound with the translation in an expensive vellum binding with silk ties. Production costs were met by subscribers, and only 250 copies were printed. The Gilbert Club ceased to exist after the publication.

DNB; Thompson and Thompson (1920); McLean (1972); Symons (1985); Ing (1986).

60. William Cecil Dampier (1867–1952)

A shorter history of science.

London, Readers Union; Cambridge University Press, 1945
x, 189 p.

In the preface to *A history of science and its relations with philosophy and religion* (1929), William Dampier indicated William Whewell's *History of the inductive sciences* (1837) and

Newton's statue on the frontispiece of William Dampier's *A shorter history of science.* Catalogue no. 60.

Philosophy of the inductive sciences (1840) as models for his enterprise. Whewell had analysed the connections between science and philosophy and Dampier thought that the time had come to reassess those relations in the light of recent scientific developments. Dampier was a Fellow of Trinity College, Cambridge; trained as a physicist, he gradually turned away from research to teaching and later to farming. In 1938 he became a member of the Cambridge History of Science Committee, which played a major role in bringing the history of science to the centre of English academia. To promote the history of science, Dampier had, with his daughter, already published *Readings in the literature of science* (1924), an anthology of passages by various 'men of science to illustrate the development of scientific thought'. His *History of science and its relations with philosophy and religion* ran to three editions before 1947.

As science was growing at full speed—in the 1947 edition Dampier referred to 'some new work especially in England and America, done to solve definite war problems', a periphrasis for the atomic bomb—so was the history of science. In revising his work, Dampier fully recognised that he had greatly benefited from the work done in the 1930s by George Sarton and others, who had substantially transformed the discipline. The audience for the history of science was also changing. In the 1930s and 1940s the subject started to be appreciated as a way to reduce excessive specialisation among would-be scientists, and courses in history of science were increasingly offered in science faculties. Publishers were also aware of a broader interest among an audience of non-scientists. In 1943 Dampier produced an abridged version of his work, in which the most difficult philosophical points would be left aside. A 'straightforward story of the growth of science reduced to its simplest terms' was made available to general readers in this slim volume of less than two hundred pages, which went through a number of reprints and editions.

DNB; Thackray (1984); Bennett (1997a); Rossiter (1999); Mayer (2000).

61. Humphrey Thomas Pledge (1903–1960)

Science since 1500. A short history of mathematics, physics, chemistry, biology. By H. T. Pledge.

London, published by His Majesty's Stationery Office, 1939 (1947 printing)
357 p.

In the 1920s the Science Museum in London in co-operation with the Ministry of Education began the production of a series of publications presenting the various collections of instruments and apparatus held in the Museum. Among such publications were descriptive catalogues including technical explanations and volumes containing the lectures given at the Museum to a general audience. To complement the growing number of publications which testified to a new public interest in scientific instruments and their history, it was decided that a more general survey on the history of science should be made available.

Science since 1500 was published in 1939. The emphasis was on science post-1800, and given the amount of technical detail, it is clear that it addressed primarily a public of 'specialists in other subjects' and university students. Brevity was secured by suppressing biographical information, usually more appealing to a lay readership. Humphrey T. Pledge was the assistant keeper of the Science Museum Library and was involved in the foundation of the British Society for the History of Science in the late 1940s. In the preface the author clearly situated his work with respect to recent publications on the same topic. He argued that, compared to books such as Dampier's *A history of science* (catalogue no. 60) which discussed science within an intellectual and philosophical background, his work meant to explain past science in the framework of human and economic factors. However, in so doing he was not following Professor Hogben, who had made 'social needs' the key element in his interpretation of science. The reference was to Lancelot Hogben's *Mathematics for the million* (1936) and *Science for the citizen* (1938), which were shaped by a Marxist interpretation of science and had a tremendous success, the former selling over half a million copies. Pledge's political agenda was certainly less resolute than Hogben's, though he acknowledged Joseph Needham, another of the left-wing scientists of the 1930s, for having read the whole book and made many suggestions.

Janson (1961); McGucken (1984); Werskey (1988).

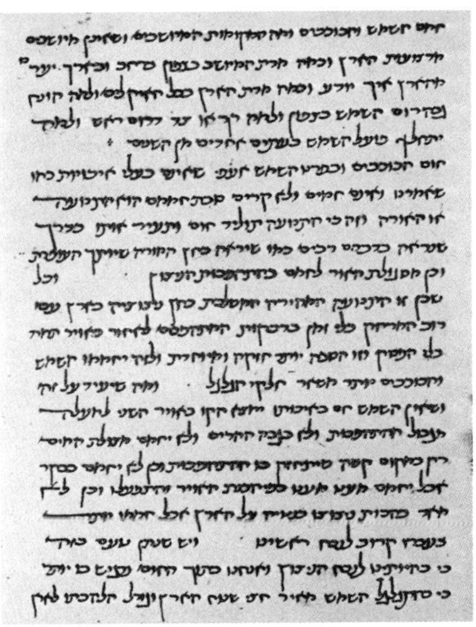

Reproduction of a thirteenth-century manuscript of science, wrongly printed upside down. Catalogue no. 61.

General view of the Royal Albert Hall during the Faraday centenary exhibition in 1931.
Catalogue no. 62.

62. Faraday centenary exhibition 23rd September to 3rd October 1931

Souvenir catalogue and guide.

[London] [printed by Oliver Burridge] [1931]
248 p.

Since the nineteenth century, anniversaries of the births and deaths of 'heroes' of science and of their discoveries have provided occasions for celebrating science and its values. These celebrations have usually included a wide range of scholarly activities, and more worldly happenings. Commemoration of national pride and commercial propaganda were often part of the message which these events aimed to convey. The centenary of Faraday's discovery of electromagnetic induction in 1931 is a case in point.

In the nineteenth century Faraday had already achieved the status of a scientific icon. When the Royal Institution, the Institution of Electrical Engineers and the Royal Society decided to celebrate the anniversary of one of his most important achievements, they spared neither time nor money to make it an unforgettable occasion. With the contributions of a number of private firms, a large-scale exhibition was mounted in the Albert Hall. The range of events was remarkable: speeches, parties, dinners and even a concert were organised over a week of intense celebrations. All the available media were used, for example a talking film with Sir William Bragg telling the story of Faraday's life was shown each day for a two-pence admission charge. Sitting at Faraday's lecture table, Bragg showed some of his famous notebooks. In the main gallery of the exhibition, a reproduction of Faraday's laboratory was constructed. Overall, though, the display of a few relics from Faraday's laboratory was overwhelmed by the exhibits celebrating the achievements of the British Electrical and Allied Manufacturers' Association, which were mainly promoting their successful electrification of the country.

Several publications made this series of remarkable but ephemeral events last. The gilt-edged catalogue and guide to the exhibition included detailed descriptions of the objects on display, explanations of their function and pictures of the Albert Hall. The edition of Faraday's multi-volume diary was already on its way, the first volume coming out in 1932. This allowed the Managers of the Royal Institution to produce an extract of the diary, have it beautifully bound, and present it as a token of appreciation to important visitors to the exhibition, including Whipple.

Cantor, Gooding and James (1991).

63. Edward Neville Da Costa Andrade (1887–1971)

Isaac Newton.

London, Max Parrish, 1950
111 p.

Since the eighteenth century the aura surrounding Newton's life and work grew and the literature on him steadily expanded. Although he was often portrayed as a solitary genius, he came to serve a variety of functions, for example as an emblem of national identity and pride. He also represented the obvious touchstone for competing ways of reconstructing the history of science.

The portrait of Newton in Da Costa Andrade's book.
Catalogue no. 63.

A successful physicist with an interest in literature, Andrade cultivated the history of science both by collecting first editions of the works of the 'great innovators in science' and by writing accessible and popular books of science; he was also involved in the meetings organised by the Cambridge History of Science Committee in 1936. In 1950 he contributed this small volume on Newton to the *Personal Portraits* series of the London publisher Max Parrish. The book became a classic: in a revised version it ran to six further editions and was translated into other languages.

One of the initial remarks with which Andrade evoked Newton's excellence to his non-specialist readers reveals how politically loaded the history of science was in the aftermath of World War II. Newton, wrote Andrade, was 'possibly the only man held in the highest esteem by the official authorities in the U.S.S.R. and by leaders of English and American thought'. Such esteem had led Russian and Anglo-American scholars to produce new editions and translations of Newton's work. At a time when the ideological and military confrontation between the two blocks was ubiquitous, and scientists' involvement in military projects stronger than ever, science was represented as an impartial enterprise above political and economical struggles. Newton, the genius free from human constraints, was transformed into an international hero.

DNB; Wallis and Wallis (1977); Wells (1983); McNeil (1988); Cantor (1997); Mayer (2000).

Robert S. Whipple as a Book Collector

One of the most important events in the transformation of the history of science into an academic discipline in Cambridge was the foundation in 1936 of the Cambridge History of Science Committee. Until World War II it was run by two scientists with a surprisingly broad approach to historical research: the physician Walter Pagel, who was studying early modern religion and magic, and the biochemist Joseph Needham, already known as an historian of embryology, who would later work on Chinese science. By 1942 both had left Cambridge and the Committee underwent major changes. Increasingly it became the turf of historians, in particular of Herbert Butterfield, whose commitment to the discipline would be driven in the 1940s and 1950s by concerns about the danger to liberal humanism of excessive scientific specialisation. Such increased sensitivity for the politics of science and its history was one legacy of the war to Cambridge dons (Bennett 1997a; Mayer 2000). But it was not the only one.

In October 1944, Robert S. Whipple, the former managing director of the Cambridge Scientific Instrument Company, bequeathed his collection of rare books and antique scientific instruments to the University of Cambridge, possibly with an honorary degree in mind. To celebrate the presentation, instruments and books were exhibited the following month, but however grateful academics claimed to be, it took a long time before they succeeded in meeting Whipple's request that the University find a suitable site to exhibit the collections, employ a curator, and make the books the core of a reference library in the Museum.[1] It was not until May 1951 that a proper museum was opened in Corn Exchange Street. Meanwhile, the books were kept in the University Library.

The history of the negotiations surrounding the establishment of the Whipple Museum in the late 1940s and early 1950s has been told several times (Bennett 1997a), but the broader network of collectors and dealers within which Whipple developed his collecting project remains to be explored. More generally, scholars researching the collecting of science relics in the twentieth century have usually concentrated on instruments, even when, as in Whipple's case, books were an integral element of his collection. Little has been done to reconstruct when and why science books became desirable objects for private collectors, or to analyse why they were sometimes transferred to public institutions.[2] By exploring the collecting activities of Robert S. Whipple, this essay tries to fill some of these gaps. It is divided into four sections. After presenting a brief biographical sketch of Whipple, in the second section I outline the broader picture of the entry of science books into the antiquarian book market in the first decades of the last century. In the third section, I home in on the much more specific network of collectors with whom Whipple was in contact. This leads me to focus on the activities of institutions such as the Optical and the Physical Societies of London, of both of which Whipple was a member. To make sense of any collecting, it is necessary to investigate those who supplied the objects, the dealers. In the fourth and final section I examine the activities of Thomas H. Court, one of Whipple's major suppliers of both instruments and books, and of Ernst Weil, with whom Whipple also did business, though on a much more limited scale. I argue that the strong link between instruments and books which we find in Whipple's circle of collectors and dealers was the distinctive feature of a broader and diverse community, the activities of which shaped research in the history of science in the first half of the century. Members of this community happily crossed boundaries between scholarship and commerce, but when the history of science became an academic discipline, and I take the end of World War II to be a landmark in this process, their contributions tended to be marginalised and were eventually effaced.

Robert S. Whipple

Robert Whipple had a life-long connection with the world of scientific instruments (Whipple 1942; *DNB*). After a period as an assistant at the Kew Observatory, he became assistant manager of L. P. Casella, one of the most important scientific instrument manufacturers in London. Later he moved to Cambridge to become the private assistant of Horace Darwin, who in 1881 had founded the Cambridge Scientific Instrument Company (CSIC) (Cattermole and Wolfe 1984).

Whipple matriculated at Trinity College in 1899 but never proceeded to a degree. Apart from his expertise in the field of scientific instruments, he brought to Cambridge his invaluable flair for business and played a vital role in running and expanding the CSIC, from 1905 as Managing Director. In those early years, the British scientific instrument industry was a relatively small trade, though well established. But a huge transformation took place during World War I, when production met the increasing demand for military supplies. Companies developed research projects and strengthened their connections with scientists working in university departments (Williams 1994). Whipple retired in 1935, and served as chairman of the board of directors of the CSIC from 1939 to 1949. He was a fellow of many scientific societies and a key supporter of the Highgate Literary and Scientific Institution in North London. In 1944 he was involved in the first discussions on the foundation of the British Society for the History of Science (BSHS), and was a member of its Council from 1952 to 1953 (Browne 1997). Shortly before his death in 1953, he was nominated vice-president of the BSHS, possibly partly due to a substantial cash donation he made to the Society to meet some legal expenses.[3]

Whipple started to collect systematically in the 1920s when he was still the busy director of the CSIC.[4] The 'annus mirabilis' for his purchases was 1927, when he bought 216 books, the majority from T. H. Court. On 19 March, for instance, he bought more than 50 books from Court. 1930 was another year of great acquisition, when Whipple purchased 162 books. Later on Whipple bought an average of 40 books per year until 1938, when he bought 99 books. Almost half of the books in the Whipple Collection come from Court and it is clear that he cultivated a very efficient relationship with this dealer. Among the antiquarian booksellers Whipple visited increasingly in the last years of his life, he favoured Davis and Orioli in London, from whom he bought 85 books. Sotheran and Malcom Gardner follow with 50 books each, and then Myers of New Bond Street with 26. At Quaritch Whipple bought only 21 books. Whipple did not despise antiquarian bookshops, but he was the kind of collector who was too busy to spend time browsing in antiquarian bookshops in search of the best purchase; so he took advantage of what Court, who neither had a shop nor published catalogues, could find and offer him. In his purchases Whipple was certainly not driven by an interest in bindings, although he would spend money on restoring volumes in poor condition. Neither was he a collector obsessed with his own image. The book-plate, which was probably only added at the time of the presentation of the collection to the University of Cambridge, is a simple name label with no decoration at all.

Collecting science books

Was there anything special about collecting science books in the first decades of the last century? In 1900, science books were not in the canon of British book collecting. Of course astronomers, natural philosophers and physicians had assembled libraries which were often more than a collection of working tools (Wells 1983; Overmier 2000). From A. N. L. Munby's research, for example, we know a good deal about the bibliographical investigations carried out by mathematicians such as George Peacock and Augustus De Morgan around the middle of the nineteenth century, as well as about their great scientific libraries (Munby 1968; Rice 1996). Furthermore, the book collecting of nineteenth- and twentieth-century physicians is a well known feature of their self-fashioning (Besson 1990). And yet we also know that De Morgan regarded himself as a pioneer and complained about the paucity of specialist booksellers and fellow collectors (Munby 1968, 12). In the preface to the *Bibliotheca Chemica*, the famous catalogue of James Young's collection of chemical and alchemical books which John Ferguson published in 1906, the concern at the lack of interest in the history of science in Britain is unequivocal (Ferguson 1906).

If one takes into account collectors who were not directly involved in scientific investigations, the picture becomes even more complex. On the one hand, it is likely that the works of national heroes such as Newton always had a secure place in nineteenth-century libraries. On the other hand, it is significant that in influential guides for book collectors, such as Thomas F. Dibdin's *The Library Companion*, science books are simply not mentioned (Dibdin 1825). A substantial section is devoted to travel literature, but the very brief references to the works of Boyle and Newton are in the section on 'Philology'. In the

1887 multi-volume general catalogue of books offered to the public by Bernard Quaritch, the first volume includes manuscripts and books related to science. A quick count of the pages devoted to the various subsections is revealing. Natural history takes a bit less than three hundred pages; physical, mathematical and applied sciences, which are grouped together, take only sixty. In the general index to the volume, Isaac Newton has six entries, Galileo Galilei three, Johannes Hevelius and Robert Hooke none, Shakespeare ninety-three (Quaritch 1887).

Throughout the nineteenth century, collecting books of science remained the province of a small number of collectors, mainly those professionally involved in scientific research who developed an interest in the history of their disciplines. Their activities as collectors had no impact on the canon of book collecting in general and their demand did not lead to the development of a specialist market. John Carter argued that in the 1920s two major trends developed, namely the vogue for contemporary English authors, and a new interest in what he defined as 'books of thought', by which he meant principally books of science (Carter 1948). This, he wrote, 'was a revolutionary departure from all the accepted canons' (Carter 1948, 53). While these books had been collected on the Continent for a long time, only recently had they caught the attention of British bibliophiles. Neither Prince Baldassarre Buoncompagni nor Pierre Duhem, who built up huge libraries of science books in the second half of the nineteenth century, had served as models for British collectors (Carter 1948, 53). Carter argued that the great example of William Osler definitively awakened the interest of British collectors in science books, although Osler's collection itself is merely another manifestation of the older tradition of collecting medical books. To find that kind of impact on the collecting of science books in general, we have to look ahead to the mid-1930s, when the books of Herbert McLean Evans, illustrating epoch-making achievements in the history of science, were exhibited at the University of California at Berkeley and a catalogue published.[5] A physician with a strong interest in first editions of science books, Evans collected with a wide scope. The exhibition was so popular that it has been held responsible for the rise in demand and in prices of books of science (Zeitlin 1971). Subsequent exhibitions of science books were modelled on it, for example the famous exhibition organised by Harrison Horblit at the Grolier Club in 1958, with a catalogue published in 1964 (Horblit 1964). An essay by the science historian I. Bernard Cohen on 'Has Science a Humanistic Value?' completed this luxurious catalogue which became an influential guide for collectors. In the preface, Horblit argued for the impact of the growing field of the history of science on patterns of collecting, and contrasted the recent situation with that prior to the 1920s when books of medicine were coveted by collectors but those of general science were 'simply ignored'. *One Hundred Books Famous in Science* was a celebration of the landmarks of science. This purpose is even clearer in *Heralds of Science*, the catalogue which the great collector Bern Dibner published in 1955. Dibner openly acknowledged the influence of Evans as his model and dedicated the book to 'the book dealers in many lands who patiently gathered, preserved, collated and catalogued our heritage of science'. The case of Dibner, who came from a working-class background to become a successful entrepreneur with a strong interest in the history of technology, is an important departure from the hitherto dominant model of collecting medical books (Dibner 1955; Holton and Schweber 1988).

If by the middle of the century the 1920s and the 1930s were seen as the time when science books emerged on to the book collecting scene, it is worth exploring how this change was recorded in contemporary sources. One of the clearest pieces of evidence of the increasing popularity of science books among a wider range of collectors is to be found in the publication of the *Bibliotheca Chemico-Mathematica*, the catalogue of the antiquarian bookshop Sotheran (Sotheran and Zeitlinger 1921–1952; see catalogue no. 56). In the preface to the 1932 volume, the compiler, Heinrich Zeitlinger (Simmons and Chidley 1982), wrote:

> When the *Bibliotheca Chemico-Mathematica* was started twenty-six years ago, the commercial outlook was by no means a bright one. The classics of exact science were then in little request and the collectors few. The undertaking of an annotated catalogue of such an extent was therefore one that promised little or no return for the amount of work and expenses involved. Later years have fully justified its inception, and it must be placed to his [Sotheran's] credit to have encouraged, for the sake of science, the undertaking in such unpromising circumstances.[6]

Again in the volume published in 1952, Zeitlinger reiterated that the price of science books had increased in the previous 30 years, with no sign of abating. And he concluded that 'at one time the cinderella of the book collector, [these volumes] now appear to have become one of his principal objects'.[7]

If Sotheran's catalogue recorded the changes in the market at the same time as it promoted them, another type of publication aimed at collectors contributed to making these changes increasingly popular. I refer to handbooks for the general collector, for example the *Book Collector's Vade Mecum* compiled by Andrew Block (Block 1938). In the preface to the second edition of his guide, Block argued that three main areas had grown enormously in the recent period: editions of musical classics, scientific works and Juvenilia. Block grouped science books under three different headings, 'Rare and Early Technical Works', 'Science and Medicine', and 'The Occult'. References to the books were often inaccurate, while the organisation of his guide seems to suggest that readers were more interested in science as a heterogeneous department of affordable books, than in the field of supposedly priceless human achievements. However, Block did point out that all the works listed were either very rare, or the outstanding works of their class, and that though not cheap, they were not exorbitantly expensive either (Block 1938, 24). While it would be interesting to know more about the public which Block was addressing, his remarks offer a snapshot of the moment in the history of book collecting when prices of science books were on the increase, but still affordable by a wide range of collectors.[8]

In the 1880s, the dispersal of collections and sales of country house libraries flooded the market with books (Carter 1948, 51–53). Among the new fashions of the early twentieth century, such as first editions of contemporary authors and eighteenth-century literature, science books started to catch the interest of collectors on an unprecedented scale. Having documented that change in this section, in the next I would like to discuss how we might explain it. I shall focus on the circumscribed community of collectors in which Robert Whipple was active and on their motives in collecting 'relics' of science.

A network of collectors

As the manager of one of the most important scientific instrument companies, Whipple was a member of several scientific societies which were important places for collaboration between instrument makers and scientists (Williams 1994, 112). He was president of the Optical Society, vice-president of the Physical Society and co-operated in the establishment of the Institute of Physics.

During World War I British scientific instrument production grew enormously, but in the early 1920s government orders fell and companies faced immense problems. The risk of losing the expertise which had been accumulated in the previous years led companies to develop various industrial strategies, but remaining competitive on the European market was a priority they all shared (Williams 1994). The Annual Exhibition of Instruments and Research Apparatus and the Annual Optical Convention which were arranged by the Physical and Optical Societies at Imperial College offered an important opportunity to check the state of the art. Reports of these events appeared regularly in the *Journal of Scientific Instruments*, on whose advisory board Whipple had sat since its foundation. During the 1920s these exhibitions became increasingly popular with the general public, who paid to enjoy the new instruments on display and attend evening lectures on various subjects. Between 1925 and the mid-1930s historical exhibits of antique instruments were arranged, and lectures focused on historical topics. Often the Science Museum lent instruments for these historical exhibitions. In 1927, the physicist Edward Neville da Costa Andrade, dressed in historical costume and a wig, performed physical demonstrations with apparatus such as an original air-pump and a replica of Francis Hauksbee's electrical machine (Andrade 1927). Optical instruments provided particularly successful demonstrations, including the projection of optical illusions to a 'large number of non technical visitors' organised by Reginald Clay and Richard Paget in April 1926.[9] Whipple himself gave a lecture on the history of the galvanometer in 1934, in which he demonstrated old instruments lent by the Science Museum (Whipple 1934).

These exhibitions met various strongly intertwined needs. While offering a location for commercial purposes, they gave scientists and instrument makers a platform from which to address a non-specialist audience. History provided them with a means to win wider public interest. As the editors of the *Journal of Scientific Instruments* frankly admitted after the success of the optical illusion shows, 'we hope that their popularity will continue and that they will have the effect of stimulating public interest in optical and other scientific subjects'.[10] Exhibiting both the latest novelties and antique objects worked in two ways to build a public image of science. While they met and strengthened the existing popular interest in inventors and the production of technical devices, they also represented and reinforced the increasingly widespread realisation that science had changed dramatically since 1900, turning its previous achievements into 'history'. Exhibiting old and new instruments side by side conveyed the message that present-day science was built upon a distinguished past and at the same time was extraordinarily innovative. It was also supposed to give the public a heightened sense of national pride.

Apart from attracting public interest by exhibiting and lecturing on antique instruments, the organisers of these exhibitions, including Da Costa Andrade and Clay, were themselves collectors of science relics. As instruments became increasingly crucial in British industry, and science increasingly bound up with commercial enterprises, collecting instruments of the past and rare books worked to reinforce a genteel identity which more mundane activities could taint, or to create such an identity in the first place (Turner, A. 1987, 1995).

Outside England, the moral value of bibliophily and collecting books of science was widely recognised among those American scientists, patrons of scientific research and scholars who in the 1920s started to sponsor and carry out investigations into the history of science (Thackray 1984). A close analysis of the patterns of collecting developed by scientists, businessmen involved in the growing trade in technology, and magnates on both sides of the Atlantic will throw further light on the motives underlying the success of rare books of science in the antiquarian market. Sometimes books were their main collecting focus, sometimes they were an integral part of wider projects centred on instruments and their role in the history of science and technology. Of course, members of this commercial network did not have a monopoly on preserving relics of science. In Great Britain, connoisseurs such as Robert T. Gunther, founder of the Museum of the History of Science in Oxford, were pursuing this aim with equal passion (Simcock 1985). Gunther's archaeology of science was, however, harshly attacked by Andrade, who questioned his scholarship in what appears to be a battle for ownership of the national scientific heritage.[11] Whipple did not take sides in this fight. While he found recognition of, and a stimulus for, his collecting in the community of businessmen and scientists around the Optical and Physical Societies, his decision to bequeath his collections to the University of Cambridge was certainly inspired by Gunther's activities (Bennett 1994).

This sketch can serve as a working framework for further research on collectors, but it is now necessary to concentrate on some other important actors, namely the dealers. In the final section I shall focus on those book dealers with whom Whipple did business.

Dealing in books and instruments

Whipple bought almost half of the books he presented in 1944 from the dealer Thomas H. Court, who is a puzzling character in the world of book and instrument collecting of the first half of the century. Highly regarded by his contemporaries, who praised his generosity and acknowledged his expertise, he was first of all a self-made man (Heywood 1951; Follett 1977, 155; Insley 1982; Turner, G. L'E. 1989, 161). He is probably best known for the deal he made with D. Baxandall, the Curator of the collection of microscopes at the Science Museum. Court would buy microscopes and other instruments, and present them to the Museum or loan them for exhibition, but on the understanding that he could always remove them, if he needed them for other reasons or if he had better items to offer in exchange (Insley 1982, 345). It would not be an exaggeration to say that Court used the museum as his warehouse.[12] Between 1913 and 1918 he also worked there part-time; his largest donations were in 1928 and in 1931. He became an authority on the history of microscopes. Between 1926 and 1930 he published several articles with Moritz von Rohr in the *Transactions of the Optical Society* and in 1932 he wrote a book on the history of microscopes jointly with Reginald Clay (Clay and Court 1932; see catalogue no. 51). Clearly, Court established himself as a successful broker in the varied world of antiquarians, museum curators and academics.[13] It was here that the strong relationship between Whipple and Court developed. Unfortunately, Court's archive is very meagre with regard to his trade in books, and how precisely he bought and sold them remains unclear.[14] At his death in 1951, his books were sold at Sotheby's and realised about £4,500.[15] Dealers are businessmen, and Court seemed to possess entrepreneurial qualities in the highest degree (Insley 1982, 350–351). While Court undoubtedly developed an expertise in microscopes, he probably never had a sound bibliographical competence. With some confidence, but also acknowledging that more research is required, we can place Court at one end of the wide sociological spectrum of book and instrument dealers.

At the opposite end we find Ernst Weil, whose life and activities offer a striking contrast to Court's. The relations between Weil and Whipple were much less strong than those between Whipple and Court. Whipple was already on the point of presenting his collection to Cambridge when Weil started his own business in 1943. Whipple had been a client of E. P. Goldschmidt, Weil's senior partner between 1933 and 1943, and they may have met at Goldschmidt's shop. Furthermore, a letter of 1951 in which Weil offered Whipple a French astrolabe proves that they retained close business links.[16]

Weil was born in Ulm of a wealthy family and came to London to study banking at the beginning of the century (Feisenberger 1965; Weil 1995). After World War I he started a doctorate in art history under the supervision of the noted art historian Professor Heinrich Wölfflin in Munich. His dissertation on fifteenth-century German woodcuts was published in 1923 (Weil 1923). Meanwhile, he had started to publish illustrated books, and then joined the firm of H. W. Täuber, an active antiquarian bookseller. Their bookshop was one of the first in Germany to specialise in early modern medicine and natural science. In 1933 Weil fled Germany and came to London, where he became Goldschmidt's partner. Weil and Goldschmidt shared a special interest in early books of science and medicine and published extremely detailed catalogues on this topic. In 1943 they split their business amicably and Weil started to trade in scientific instruments as well as books. He maintained close relationships with book dealers on the Continent, where he travelled regularly. He was very much interested in alchemy and the history of chemistry, and in 1949 published the *Bibliotheca Alchemica et Chemica*, an annotated catalogue of the library of Denis Duveen.[17] As an active member of the Antiquarian Booksellers Association, as well as of the Bibliographical Society, Weil contributed several articles and reviews to *The Book Collector* and *The Library*. In 1949, he gave a lecture on science books, the fascinating reflections of a learned book dealer on the new and growing field of the history of science. He realised that collectors had only recently turned to science books, and was aware that these challenged the traditional criteria of bibliophily. For instance, a copy in poor condition but full of annotations was certainly more valuable than an elegantly bound copy (Weil 1952, 78). Furthermore, Weil stressed the enormous importance of reconstructing libraries belonging to past scientists. After paying homage to Zeitlinger, whom he regarded as a pioneer, he set a fascinating agenda for antiquarian booksellers who wanted to specialise in science books. Their challenging task would be nothing less than the documentation and preservation of the sources of the history of science. These were not just the great classical books, but also minor works and papers, which historians had probably not yet learnt to appreciate, but might one day find of interest (Weil 1952, 83–84). Weil's tips to young colleagues show an exceptionally acute awareness of a major question in the newly established field of the history of science. Feisenberger's obituary of Weil turned upside down the received view that science books became popular as a result of the establishment of the history of science as an academic discipline. Feisenberger argued for the role played by those who, like Weil, were able to draw the attention of scholars to the value of hitherto neglected sources. It was thanks to them that the history of science had become of major interest in the learned world (Feisenberger 1965, 163).

While I have traced the activities of Court among scientists, museum curators and instrument makers, Weil was particularly at home in the rarefied atmosphere of scholars developing the discipline of bibliography. But the business which each of them conducted contributed in different ways to providing the history of science with its most important sources: books and instruments.

The foundation of the British Society for the History of Science in 1947 began the process of the professionalization of the discipline (Cantor 1997). Yet, from the correspondence of its first Secretary, Francis Butler, it is clear that for some of its members the Society was to provide a stage where people with different backgrounds could meet and discuss. The businessman and collector Robert Whipple was a founding member, and antiquarian book dealers such as Weil and Feisenberger were soon invited to join.[18]

Later scholars have dismissed or forgotten the contribution of dealers and their clients to the history of science. By investigating Robert Whipple's collecting projects and the circles in which he was active, we can start to identify these actors and reconstruct their activities. Standing at the intersection of trade, connoisseurship and academy, they shaped both the history of book collecting and the history of science.

Notes

1 *Cambridge University Reporter*, 75 (1944), 158.
2 Research has concentrated on the profile of the collections rather than how they were assembled and donated. See, for example, Wood and Golinski (1981).
3 On 26 January 1953 Whipple offered £100 towards the cost of incorporation of the BSHS. See Science Museum Library, Archive of the BSHS, 1 (Foundation records).
4 Whipple kept an accession register of his purchases, from which the following information is taken. The register is now in the Whipple Museum.
5 *Exhibition* (1934).
6 Sotheran and Zeitlinger (1932), ix; one of Zeitlinger's major scoops was the acquisition of part of Newton's library. The history of these books, which remained for more than twenty years in the warehouse of Sotheran's is also a telling episode in the relations between book collecting and the history of science (Zeitlinger 1944; Harrison 1978).
7 Sotheran and Zeitlinger (1952), [v].
8 To chart the rising prices of science books is beyond the scope of this essay. The accessibility of the first edition of Newton's *Principia* as late as the 1920s is apparent in Harrison Horblit's recollection that a copy had been sold in 1921 for $80, the same price as a copy of the bibliography of Blake by Geoffrey Keynes (Horblit 1964, 3).
9 Reviewed in the *Journal of Scientific Instruments* 3 (1925–26), 252–53.
10 *Journal of Scientific Instruments* 3 (1925–26), 253.
11 A vitriolic review of Gunther's edition of the diary of Robert Hooke was published by Andrade in *Nature* 137 (1936), 378–81 and 703.
12 This practice was, however, widespread; the Science Museum was seen as a transitory home for objects by various instrument manufacturers.
13 In thanking Court for the loan of some instruments in 1922, Alan Pollard, who was Professor of Optical Engineering at Imperial College and manager of an electrical company, hoped that this would be just the beginning of a joint research project. See Science Museum Library, Court Archive, Correspondence with the Optical Society E/1.
14 An old ledger which Court recycled by sticking in clippings of book catalogues and a couple of letters from Gunther and Whipple about the purchase of books dated respectively 1925 and 1939 are among the few pieces of evidence of Court's activities as a book dealer I have found so far. See Science Museum Library, Court Archive, W/2; J; I/1. Most of the correspondence kept in this Archive concerns Court as an instrument dealer.
15 See the catalogue of Sotheby's, 1951, 17 December and following day, 'A Remarkable Collection of Early Scientific Books. The property of Thomas Henry Court, Esq'.
16 Whipple Museum Papers, Folder D/59.
17 *Bibliotheca Alchemica et Chemica* (1949).
18 See the letters from Feisenberger, J. I. Davis, and E. Maggs to Butler accepting the invitation to subscribe, and the list of members including the name of Weil, in the Archive of the BSHS, 3/3.

Bibliography

Abbreviations

BJHS *The British Journal for the History of Science*

DBI *Dizionario Biografico degli Italiani.* Rome: Istituto della Enciclopedia Italiana, 1960–

DNB *The Dictionary of National Biography.* Oxford: Oxford University Press, 1917–1996

DSB *Dictionary of Scientific Biography*, edited by Charles C. Gillispie, 8 vols. New York: Charles Scribner's Sons, 1981

Adams, T.R. (1993) 'Mount and Page. Publishers of Eighteenth-Century Maritime Books', in *A Potencie of Life. Books in Society. The Clark Lectures 1986–1987,* edited by N. Barker, 145–177. London: The British Library.

Adams, T.R., and D.W. Waters (1995) *English Maritime Books Printed before 1801. Relating to Ships, Their Construction and Their Operation at Sea. Including Articles in the 'Philosophical Transactions of the Royal Society' and the 'Transactions of the American Philosophical Society'.* Providence: The John Carter Brown Library; Greenwich: The National Maritime Museum.

Alexander, A.F.O'D. (1981) 'Dreyer, Johann Louis Emile', in *DSB*, vol. 3 & 4.

Allen, C.J. (1953) *A Century of Scientific Instrument Making 1853–1953.* London: Published for W.F. Stanley & Co. by Harley Publishing Co.

Allen, D. [1976] (1994) *The Naturalist in Britain. A Social History.* Princeton: Princeton University Press.

Altick, R.D. (1957) *The English Common Reader. A Social History of the Mass Reading Public, 1800–1900.* Chicago: The University of Chicago Press.

Anderson, R.G.W., J. Burnett, and B. Gee (eds) (1990) *Handlist of Scientific Instrument-Makers' Trade Catalogues 1600–1914.* Edinburgh: National Museums of Scotland, in association with the Science Museum.

Anderson, R.G.W. (1995) 'Connoisseurship, pedagogy or antiquarianism? What were instruments doing in nineteenth-century national collections in Great Britain?', *Journal of the History of Collections* 7, 211–225.

Andrade, E.N. Da Costa (1927) 'A lecture with experiments on various subjects giving an account of several surprising phenomena touching light and electricity', *Journal of Scientific Instruments* 4, 130–137.

Argles, M. (1964) *South Kensington to Robbins. An Account of English Technical and Scientific Education since 1851.* London: Longmans.

Auerbach, J.A. (1999) *The Great Exhibition of 1851. A Nation on Display.* New Haven: Yale University Press.

Augarde, J.D. (1989) 'La fabrication des instruments scientifiques du XVIIIe siècle et la corporation des fondeurs', in *Studies in the History of Scientific Instruments. Papers Presented at the 7th Symposium of the Scientific Instrument Commission of the Union Internationale d'Histoire et de Philosophie des Sciences, Paris 15–19 September 1987,* edited by C. Blondel, F. Parot, A. Turner, and M. Williams, 52–72. London: Rogers Turner Book.

Bailey, A. (1995) 'Units, Standards and Constants', in *Twentieth Century Physics,* edited by L.M. Brown, A. Pais, and B. Pippard, vol. 2, 1233–1278. Bristol and Philadelphia: Institute of Physics Publishing; New York: American Institute of Physics Press.

Barnard, J., and M. Bell (1991) 'The inventory of Henry Bynneman (1583): a preliminary survey', *Publishing History* 29, 5–46.

Barocas, C., A. Ingegno, and D. Caccamo (1972) 'Burattini, Tito Livio', in *DBI*, vol. 15.

Bassy, A. (1990) 'Le texte et l'image', in *Histoire de l'édition française*, edited by R. Chartier, and J.H. Martin, vol. 2, *Le livre triumphant. 1660–1830*, 173–200. Paris: Fayard/Promodis.

Bennett, H.S. (1965) *English Books and Readers 1558 to 1603. Being a Study in the History of the Book Trade in the Reign of Elizabeth I.* Cambridge: Cambridge University Press.

Bennett, H.S. (1970) *English Books and Readers 1603 to 1640. Being a Study in the History of the Book Trade in the Reigns of James I and Charles I.* Cambridge: Cambridge University Press.

Bennett, J.A., and O. Brown (1982) *The Compleat Surveyor.* Cambridge: Whipple Museum of the History of Science.

Bennett, J.A. (1985) 'Instrument Makers and the "Decline of Science in England": The Effect of Institutional Change on the Élite Makers of the Early Nineteenth Century', in *Nineteenth-Century Scientific Instruments and Their Makers. Papers Presented at the Fourth Scientific Instrument Symposium, Amsterdam 23–26 October 1984*, edited by P.R. de Clercq, 13–27. Amsterdam: Rodopi.

Bennett, J.A. (1987) *The Divided Circle. A History of Instruments for Astronomy, Navigation and Surveying.* Oxford: Phaidon, Christie's.

Bennett, J.A. (1989) 'The social history of the microscope', *Journal of Microscopy* 155, 267–280.

Bennett, J.A. (1991) 'Geometry and surveying in early-seventeenth-century England', *Annals of Science* 48, 345–354.

Bennett, J.A., and D. Bertoloni Meli (1994) *Sphaera Mundi. Astronomy Books 1478–1600. A 50th Anniversary Exhibition at the Whipple Museum of the History of Science.* Cambridge: Whipple Museum of the History of Science.

Bennett, J.A. (1994) 'The Cambridge Legacy of Robert T. Gunther', in *Learning, Language and Inventions. Essays Presented to Francis Maddison*, edited by W.D. Hackmann, and A. Turner, 78–83. Aldershot: Variorum; Paris: Société Internationale de l'Astrolabe.

Bennett, J.A., and S. Johnston (1996) *The Geometry of War. 1500–1750. Catalogue of the Exhibition.* Oxford: Museum of the History of Science.

Bennett, J.A. (1997a) 'Museums and the establishment of the history of science at Oxford and Cambridge', *BJHS* 30, 29–46.

Bennett, J.A. (1997b) 'The instrument trade in Britain', review of *Directory of British Scientific Instrument Makers 1550–1851*, by Gloria Clifton, *Annals of Science* 54, 197–206.

Bennett, J.A. (1998) 'Practical geometry and operative knowledge', *Configurations* 6, 195–222.

Benzing, J. (1962) *Jacob Köbel zu Oppenheim 1494–1533. Bibliographie seiner Drucke und Schriften.* Wiesbaden: Guido Pressler.

Besson, A. (1990) 'Private Medical Libraries', in *Thornton's Medical Books, Libraries and Collectors. A Study of Bibliography and the Book Trade in Relation to the Medical Sciences*, edited by A. Besson, 267–300. Aldershot: Gower Publishing Company.

Biagioli, M. (1992), 'Scientific Revolution, Social Bricolage, and Etiquette', in *The Scientific Revolution in National Context*, edited by R. Porter, and M. Teich, 11–54. Cambridge: Cambridge University Press.

Bibliotheca Alchemica et Chemica: an Annotated Catalogue of Printed Books on Alchemy, Chemistry and Cognate Subjects in the Library of Denis I. Duveen. London: E. Weil, 1949.

Bierens de Haan, D. (1960) *Bibliographie Néerlandaise historique-scientifique des ouvrages importants dont les auteurs sont nés aux 16e, 17e, et 18e siècles, sur les sciences mathématiques et physiques, avec leurs applications*, Nieuwkoop: B. De Graaf.

Block, A. (1938; 1st edition 1932) *The Book Collector's Vade Mecum.* London: The Mitre Press.

Bolzoni, L. (1995) *La stanza della memoria. Modelli letterari e iconografici nell'età della stampa.* Turin: Einaudi.

Bracegirdle, B. (1978) *A History of Microtechnique. The Evolution of the Microtome and the Development of Tissue Preparation.* London: Heinemann.

Brain, R. (1994) 'Going to the Exhibition', in *The Physics of Empire. Public Lectures*, edited by R. Staley, 113–142. Cambridge: Whipple Museum of the History of Science.

Brenni, P. (1989) 'The Illustrated Catalogues of Scientific Instrument-Makers', in *Studies in the History of Scientific Instruments. Papers Presented at the 7th Symposium of the Scientific Instrument Commission of the Union Internationale d'Histoire et de Philosophie des Sciences, Paris 15–19 September 1987,* edited by C. Blondel, F. Parot, A. Turner, and M. Williams, 169–178. London: Rogers Turner Book.

Brewer, J. (1989) *The Sinews of Power. War, Money and the English State 1688–1783.* London: Unwin Hyman.

Brock, W.H. (1989) 'Patronage and publishing: journals of microscopy 1839–1989', *Journal of Microscopy* 155, 249–266.

Brockliss, L.W.B. (1987) *French Higher Education in the Seventeenth and Eighteenth Centuries. A Cultural History.* Oxford: Clarendon Press; New York: Oxford University Press.

Browne, J. (1997) 'Officers and council members of the British Society for the History of Science, 1947–97', *BJHS* 30, 77–90.

Bryden, D. (1974) 'A patchery and confusion of disjointed stuffe: Richard Delamain's *Grammelogia* of 1631/3', *Transactions of the Cambridge Bibliographical Society* VI, 158–166.

Bryden, D. (1992) 'Evidence from advertising for mathematical instrument making in London, 1556–1714', *Annals of Science* 49, 301–336.

Bryden, D. (1997a) 'Capital in the London publishing trade: Moxon's stock disposal of 1698', *The Library* 19, 293–350.

Bryden, D. (1997b) 'The instrument-maker and the printer: paper instrument made in seventeenth century London', *Bulletin of the Scientific Instrument Society* 55, 3–15.

Bryden, D. (1999) 'From 16th Century London to 19th Century Philadelphia. A peregrination through three centuries of instrument advertising and ephemera', *Bulletin of the Scientific Instrument Society* 61, 4–10.

Calvert, H. R. (1971) *Scientific Trade Cards in the Science Museum Collection.* London: Her Majesty's Stationery Office.

Cantor, G., D. Gooding, and F.A.J.L. James (1991) *Faraday.* Houndmill and London: Macmillan Education.

Cantor, G. (1997) 'Charles Singer and the early years of the British Society for the History of Science', *BJHS* 30, 5–23.

Capp, B. (1979) *Astrology and the Popular Press. English Almanacs 1500–1800.* London: Faber.

Carli, A., and A. Favaro [1896] (1972) *Bibliografia Galileiana (1568–1895).* Bologna: Libreria Antiquaria Brighenti.

Carlino, A. (1999) *Paper Bodies: A Catalogue of Anatomical Fugitive Sheets 1538–1687.* (*Medical History,* Supplement No. 19). London: Wellcome Institute for the History of Medicine.

Carter, J. (1948) *Taste and Technique in Book-Collecting. A Study of Recent Developments in Great Britain and the United States.* Cambridge: At the University Press.

Casciato, M., M.G. Ianniello, and M. Vitale (eds) (1986) *Enciclopedismo in Roma barocca: Athanasius Kircher e il Museo del Collegio Romano tra Wunderkammer e museo scientifico.* Venice: Marsilio Editori.

Cattermole, M.J.G., and A.F. Wolfe (1984) *Horace Darwin's Shop. A History of the Cambridge Scientific Instrument Company 1878–1968.* Bristol & Boston: Adam Hilger.

Chapman, A. (1990) *Dividing the Circle. The Development of Critical Angular Measurement in Astronomy 1500–1850.* New York: Ellis Horwood.

Chapman, A. (1993) 'Scientific Instruments and Industrial Innovation: the Achievement of Jesse Ramsden', in *Making Instruments Count: Essays on Historical Scientific Instruments Presented to Gerard L'Estrange Turner,* edited by R.G.W Anderson, J.A. Bennett, and W.F. Ryan, 418–430. Aldershot: Ashgate.

Chartier, R. (1987) *The Cultural Uses of Print in Early Modern France.* Princeton: Princeton University Press.

Clay, R., and T.H. Court (1932) *The History of the Microscope Compiled from Original Instruments and Documents, up to the Introduction of the Achromatic Microscope.* London: Charles Griffin and Company.

Clifton, G. (1995) *Directory of British Scientific Instrument Makers 1550–1851. General Editor G.L'E. Turner.* London: Zwemmer in association with the National Maritime Museum.

Crawforth, M.A. (1985) 'Evidence from trade cards for the scientific instrument industry', *Annals of Science* 42, 453–544.

Darnton, R. (1991) 'History of Reading', in *New Perspectives on Historical Writing,* edited by P. Burke, 140–167. Cambridge: Polity.

Daumas, M. (1972) *Scientific Instruments of the Seventeenth and Eighteenth Centuries and Their Makers.* London: Batsford.
Debus, A. (ed.) (1968) *World Who's Who in Science. A Biographical Dictionary of Notable Scientists from Antiquity to the Present.* Chicago: Marquis-Who's Who Incorporated.
De Clercq, P.R. (1997) *At the Sign of the Oriental Lamp. The Musschenbroek Workshop in Leiden, 1660–1750.* Rotterdam: Erasmus Publishing.
De Graeve, J. (1982) 'Bibliographie d'Henri Michel', *Ciel et Terre,* Supplément au numéro de Mai-Juin 1982, 6–24.
Dibdin, T.F. (1825) *The Library Companion; Or, the Young Man's Guide and the Old Man's Comfort, in the Choice of a Library.* London: Printed for Harding, Triphook and Lepard.
Dibner, B. (1955) *Heralds of Science as Represented by Two Hundred Epochal Books and Pamphlets Selected from the Burndy Library.* Norwalk Conn.: Burndy Library.
Dörries, M. (1994) 'Balances, spectroscopes, and the reflexive nature of experiment', *Studies in History and Philosophy of Science* 25, 1–36.
Drake, S. (1978) *Galileo at Work. His Scientific Biography.* Chicago: The University of Chicago Press.
Dreyer, J.L.E. [1890] (1963) *Tycho Brahe. A Picture of Scientific Life and Work in the Sixteenth Century.* New York: Dover Publications.
Eden, P. (ed.) (1975–1976) *Dictionary of Land Surveyors and Local Cartographers of Great Britain and Ireland 1550–1850.* Folkestone: Dawson.
Eisenstein, E.L. (1983) *The Printing Revolution in Early Modern Europe.* Cambridge: Cambridge University Press.
Ernst, G. (1998) 'Gallucci, Giovannni Paolo', in *DBI,* vol. 51.
Exhibition of First Editions of Epochal Achievements in the History of Science, June 18–23 1934. Berkeley: University of California Press, 1934.
Fara, P. (1995) '"A treasure of hidden vertues": the attraction of magnetic marketing', *BJHS* 28, 5–35.
Farrell, M. (1981) 'Schumacher, Heinrich Christian', in *DSB,* vol. 11 & 12.
Feather, J. (1988) *A History of British Publishing.* London: Routledge.
Feingold, M. (1984) *The Mathematicians' Apprenticeship. Science, Universities and Society in England, 1560–1640.* Cambridge: Cambridge University Press.
Feisenberger, H.A. (1965), 'Ernst Weil', *The Book Collector* 14, 160–164.
Ferguson, J. (1906) 'Preface', in *Bibliotheca Chemica. A Catalogue of the Alchemical, Chemical and Pharmaceutical Books in the Collection of the Late James Young,* edited by J. Ferguson, vii–xxi. Glasgow: James Maclehose and Sons.
Findlen, P. (1994) *Possessing Nature. Museums, Collecting, and Scientific Culture in Early Modern Italy.* Berkeley & Los Angeles: University of California Press.
Follett, D. (1977) *The Rise of the Science Museum under Henry Lyons.* London: Science Museum.
Fyfe, A.K. (2000) *Industrial Conversion: the Religious Tract Society and Popular Science Publishing in Victorian Britain,* Ph. D. Thesis, University of Cambridge.
Galilei, G. [1890–1909] (1964–1968) *Le Opere di Galileo Galilei,* edited by A. Favaro, Florence: S.A.G. Barbéra Editore.
Galilei, G. (1978) *Operations of the Geometric and Military Compass. Translated, with an introduction by Stillman Drake.* Washington: Smithsonian Institution Press.
Galluzzi, P. (1981) 'L'Accademia del Cimento: "gusti" del principe, filosofia e ideologia dell'esperimento', *Quaderni Storici* 16, 788–844.
Gariepy, T.P. (1999) 'John Farquhar Fulton and the History of Science Society', in *Catching Up With the Vision. Essays on the Occasion of the 75th Anniversary of the Founding of the History of Science Society,* edited by M. W. Rossiter. A Supplement to *Isis* 90, 7–27.
Gascoigne, J. (1989) *Cambridge in the Age of Enlightenment. Science, Religion and Politics from the Restoration to the French Revolution.* Cambridge: Cambridge University Press.
Gingerich, O. (1993) 'Astronomical Paper Instruments with Moving Parts', in *Making Instruments Count: Essays*

on Historical Scientific Instruments Presented to Gerard L'Estrange Turner, edited by R.G.W Anderson, J.A. Bennett, and W.F. Ryan, 63–74. Aldershot: Ashgate.

Golinski, J. (1999) 'Barometers of Change: Meteorological Instruments as Machines of Enlightenment', in *The Sciences in Enlightened Europe,* edited by W. Clark, J. Golinski, and S. Schaffer, 69–93. Chicago: The University of Chicago Press.

Gooday, G. (1991) '"Nature" in the laboratory: domestication and discipline with the microscope in Victorian life science', *BJHS* 24, 307–341.

Goodison, N. (1969) *English Barometers. A History of Domestic Barometers and Their Makers.* London: Cassell.

Gouk, P. (1988) *The Ivory Sundials of Nuremberg 1500–1700.* Cambridge: Whipple Museum of the History of Science.

Grabiner, J.V. (1998) '"Some disputes of consequence": Maclaurin among the molasses barrels', *Social Studies of Science* 28, 139–168.

Grafton, A., and L. Jardine (1990), '"Studied for Action": how Gabriel Harvey read his Livy', *Past and Present* 129, 30–78.

Grzybkowska, T. (1979) *Andrzej Stech malarz gdański.* Warszawa: Państwowe Wydawnictwo Naukowe.

Guerlac, H. (1981) 'Hauksbee, Francis', in *DSB,* vol. 5 & 6.

Guglielmotti, A. (1882) *La squadra permanente della marina romana. Storia dal 1573 al 1644.* Rome: Voghera Carlo.

Guicciardini, N. (1989) *The Development of Newtonian Calculus in Britain 1700–1800.* Cambridge: Cambridge University Press.

Gunther, A.E. (1967) *Robert Gunther: a Pioneer in the History of Science, 1859–1940.* Vol XV of *Early Science in Oxford,* by R.T. Gunther. Oxford: Printed for the Subscribers.

Gunther, R.T. (1932) *The Astrolabes of the World. Based Upon the Series of Instruments in the Lewis Evans Collection in the Old Ashmolean Museum at Oxford.* Oxford: The University Press.

Gunther, R.T. (1937) *Early Science in Cambridge.* Oxford: Printed for the Subscribers.

Hackenberg, M. (1986) 'Books in artisan homes of sixteenth-century Germany', *The Journal of Library History* 21, 72–91.

Hackmann, W.D. (1985) 'The Nineteenth-Century Trade in Natural Philosophy Instruments in Britain', in *Nineteenth-Century Scientific Instruments and Their Makers. Papers Presented at the Fourth Scientific Instrument Symposium, Amsterdam 23–26 October 1984,* edited by P.R. de Clercq, 53–91. Amsterdam: Rodopi.

Hall, A.R. (1981) ''s Gravesande, Willem Jacob', in *DSB,* vol. 5 & 6.

Hankins, T.L., and R.J. Silverman (1995) *Instruments and the Imagination.* Princeton: Princeton University Press.

Harrison, J. (1978) *The Library of Isaac Newton.* Cambridge: Cambridge University Press.

Heal, A. (1925) *London Tradesmen's Cards of the XVIII Century. An Account of Their Origin and Use.* London: B.T. Batsford.

Heninger, S.K. (1977) 'Oronce Finé and English Textbooks for the Mathematical Sciences', in *Studies in the Continental Background of Renaissance English Literature: Essays Presented to John L. Lievsay,* edited by D.B.J. Randall, and G.W. Williams, 171–185. Durham, N. C.: Duke University Press.

Heywood, H. (1951) 'Thomas H. Court', *Nature* 167, 969.

Heywood, H. (1969) 'Clay and Court. Pioneer collectors of microscopes', *Microscopy. The Journal of the Queckett Microscopical Society* 31, 109–112.

Hill, K. (1998) '"Juglers or Schollers?": negotiating the role of a mathematical practitioner', in *BJHS* 31, 253–274.

Hillard, D., and E. Poulle (1971) 'Oronce Fine et l'horloge planétaire de la Bibliothèque Sainte-Geneviève', *Bibliothèque d'Humanisme et Renaissance* 33, 311–351.

Hirsch, R. (1967) *Printing, Selling and Reading 1450–1550.* Wiesbaden: Harrassowitz.

Hoge, E. (1982) 'Henri Michel', *Ciel et Terre,* Supplément au numéro de Mai-Juin 1982, 3–5.

Holmes, G. (1982) *Augustan England. Professions, State and Society, 1680–1730.* London: George Allen & Unwin.

Holton, G., and S.S. Schweber (1988) 'Bern Dibner, 1878–1988', *Isis* 79, 475–477.

Hook, D.H., and J.M. Norman (1991) *The Haskell F. Norman Library of Science & Medicine*. San Francisco: Jeremy Norman & Co. Inc.

Horblit, H.D. (1964) *One Hundred Books Famous in Science. Based on an Exhibition held at the Grolier Club*. New York: The Grolier Club.

Hudson, D., and K.W. Luckhurst (1954) *The Royal Society of Arts, 1754–1954*. London: Murray.

Ing, J. (1986) 'A London shop of the 1850s: the Chiswick Press', *Papers of the Bibliographical Society of America* 8, 153–178.

Insley, J. (1982) 'Court, Crisp and Clay. Some notes on collectors and collections of antique microscopes', *Microscopy* 34, 345–353.

Insley, J. (1984) 'Sir Frank Crisp, Baronet (1843–1919)', *Microscopy* 35, 10–24.

Inwards, R. (ed.) (1911) *William Ford Stanley. His Life and Work*. London: Crosby Lockwood & Co.

Jacomi, B. (1995) 'Du cabinet au Conservatoire. Les instruments scientifiques du Conservatoire des Arts et Métiers à Paris', *Journal of the History of Collections* 7, 227–233.

Janson, S.E. (1961) 'Humphrey Thomas Pledge', *Nature* 189, 357.

Johns, A. (1998) *The Nature of the Book. Print and Knowledge in the Making*. Chicago: The University of Chicago Press.

Johnston, S., F. Willmoth, and J.A. Bennett (1985) *The Grounde of Artes. Mathematical Books of 16th-century England*. Cambridge: Whipple Museum of the History of Science.

Johnston, S. (1991) 'Mathematical practitioners and instruments in Elizabethan England', *Annals of Science* 48, 319–344.

Johnston, S. (1994) *Making Mathematical Practice. Gentlemen, Practitioners and Artisans in Elizabethan England*. Ph. D. Thesis, University of Cambridge.

Kenney, C. E. (1950) 'William Leybourn, 1626–1716', *The Library* V, 159–171.

Killy, W., and R. Vierhaus (eds) (1998) *Deutsche Biographische Enzyclopädie*, vol. 8. Munich: K. G. Saur.

King, H.C., and J.R. Millburn (1978) *Geared to the Stars. The Evolution of Planetariums, Orreries, and Astronomical Clocks*. Bristol: Adam Hilger Ltd.

Kusukawa, S. (2000) 'Incunables and Sixteenth-Century Books', in *Thornton and Tully's Scientific Books, Libraries and Collectors. A Study of Bibliography and the Book Trade in Relation to the History of Science*, edited by A. Hunter, 115–163. Aldershot: Ashgate.

Lecoq, B. (1991) 'L'édition et la science', in *Histoire de l'édition française*, edited by R. Chartier, and J.H. Martin, vol. 4, *Le livre concurrencé 1900–1950*, 332–341. Paris: Fayard/Promodis.

Le Fanu, W. (1962) 'John Fulton's historical and bibliographical work', *Journal of the History of Medicine and Allied Sciences* 17, 38–71.

Licoppe, C. (1996) *La formation de la pratique scientifique. Le discours de l'expérience en France et en Angleterre (1630–1820)*. Paris: Découverte.

Lindberg, S.G. (1979) 'Mobiles in books: volvelles, inserts, pyramids, divinations and children's games', *The Private Library* 2, 49–82.

Long, P. (1991a) 'The openess of knowledge: an ideal and its context in 16th-century writing on mining and metallurgy', *Technology and Culture* 32, 318–355.

Long, P. (1991b) 'Invention, authorship, "intellectual property", and the origins of patents: notes toward a conceptual history', *Technology and Culture* 32, 846–884.

Lowood, H., and R. Rider (1994) 'Literary technology and typographic culture: the instrument of print in early modern science', *Perspectives on Science* 2, 1–37.

Manguel, A. (1996) *A History of Reading*. London: Flamingo.

Margolin, J.C. (1976) 'L'enseignement des mathèmatiques en France (1540–70) Charles de Bovelles, Fine, Peletier, Ramus', in *French Renaissance Studies 1540–70: Humanism and the Encyclopedia*, edited by P. Scharrat, 109–55. Edinburgh: Edinburgh University Press.

Mayer, Anna-K. (2000) 'Setting up a discipline: conflicting agendas of the Cambridge History of Science Committee, 1936–1950', *Studies in History and Philosophy of Science* 31A (4), in press.

McConnell, A. (1985) 'Nineteenth-century geomagnetic instruments and their makers', in *Nineteenth-Century*

Scientific Instruments and Their Makers. Papers Presented at the Fourth Scientific Instrument Symposium, Amsterdam 23–26 October 1984, edited by P.R. de Clercq, 29–52. Amsterdam: Rodopi.

McGucken, W. (1984) *Scientists, Society, and State. The Social Relations of Science Movement in Great Britain 1931–1947.* Columbus: Ohio State University Press.

McKerrow, R.B. (ed.) (1910) *A Dictionary of Printers and Booksellers in England, Scotland and Ireland, and of Foreign Printers of English Books 1557–1640.* London: Printed for the Bibliographical Society.

McKerrow, R.B. (1913) *Printers' and Publishers' Devices in England & Scotland 1485–1640.* London: Printed for the Bibliographical Society.

McKitterick, D. (1998) *A History of Cambridge University Press.* Vol. 2, *Scholarship and Commerce 1698–1872.* Cambridge: Cambridge University Press.

McLean, R. (1972) *Victorian Book Design and Colour Printing.* London: Faber & Faber.

McNeil, M. (1988) 'Newton as a National Hero', in *Let Newton be!*, edited by J. Fauvel et al., 223–239. Oxford: Oxford University Press.

Mercier, A. (1994) *Un conservatoire pour les arts et métiers.* Paris: Gallimard.

Middleton, W.E.K. (1964) *The History of the Barometer.* Baltimore: Johns Hopkins University Press.

Middleton, W.E.K. (1971) *The Experimenters. A Study of the Accademia del Cimento.* Baltimore: Johns Hopkins University Press.

Middleton, W.E.K. (1975) 'More light on the publication of the "Saggi di Naturali Esperienze fatte nell'Accademia del Cimento"', *Studi Secenteschi* 16, 219–230.

Millburn, J.R. (1976) *Benjamin Martin. Author, Instrument-maker, and 'Country Showman'.* Leyden: Noordhoff International Publishing.

Millburn, J.R. (2000) *Adams of Fleet Street, Instrument Makers to King George III.* Aldershot: Ashgate.

Monaco, G. (1998) 'Alcune considerazioni sul "Maximus Tubus" di Hevelius', *Nuncius* 13, 533–550.

Morton, A.Q., and J.A. Wess (1993) *Public & Private Science. The King George III Collection.* Oxford: Oxford University Press in association with the Science Museum.

Muirhead, A. (1962) 'Portrait of a bibliophile IX: John Farquhar Fulton, 1899–1960', *The Book Collector* 11, 427–436.

Munby, A.N.L. (1968) *The History and Bibliography of Sciences in England: The First Phase 1833–1845.* Berkeley & Los Angeles: University of California.

Nevett, T.R. (1982) *Advertising in Britain. A History.* London: Heinemann.

Nielsen, A.V. (1981) 'Schjellerup, Hans Carl Frederik Christian', in *DSB*, vol. 11 & 12.

Nummedal, T., and P. Findlen (2000) 'Words of Nature: Scientific Books in the Seventeenth Century', in *Thornton and Tully's Scientific Books, Libraries and Collectors. A Study of Bibliography and the Book Trade in Relation to the History of Science*, edited by A. Hunter, 164–215. Aldershot: Ashgate.

O'Malley, J. (ed.) (1999) *The Jesuits: Cultures, Sciences, and the Arts, 1540–1773.* Toronto: University of Toronto Press.

Overmier, J. (2000) 'Scientific Book Collectors and Collections, Public and Private, 1720 to Date', in *Thornton and Tully's Scientific Books, Libraries and Collectors. A Study of Bibliography and the Book Trade in Relation to the History of Science*, edited by A. Hunter, 367–391. Aldershot: Ashgate.

Pagnini, P. (1942) 'Avvertimento', in *Le opere dei discepoli di Galileo Galilei. Edizione Nazionale*, edited by G. Abetti, and P. Pagnini. Vol. 1, *L'Accademia del Cimento.* Florence: S.A.G. Barbéra Editore.

Pantin, I. (1988) 'Les problèmes de l'édition des livres scientifiques: l'exemple de Guillaume Cavellat', in *Le livre dans l'Europe de la Renaissance. Actes du XXVIIIe colloque international d' ètudes humanistes de Tours,* edited by P. Aquilon, and H.J. Martin, 240–251. Paris: Promodis.

Paul, H.W. (1980) 'The Role and Reception of the Monograph in Nineteenth-Century French Science', in *Development of Science Publishing in Europe*, edited by A.J. Meadows, 123–148. Amsterdam: Elsevier Science Publishers.

Payen, F. (1981) 'Bion, Nicolas', in *DSB*, vol. 1 & 2.

Plomer, H.R. (1907), *A Dictionary of the Booksellers and Printers Who Were at Work in England, Scotland and Ireland from 1641 to 1667.* London: Printed for the Bibliographical Society.

Poggendorff, J.C. (1863) *Biographisch-Literarisches Handwörterbuch zur Geschichte der Exacten Wissenschaften.* Leipzig: Verlag von Johann Ambrosius Barth.

Pollard, A.W., and Redgrave, G.R. (1986) *A Short-Title Catalogue of Books Printed in England, Scotland, & Ireland and of English Books Printed Abroad 1475–1640. Second Edition, Revised and Enlarged by W. A. Jackson and F. S. Ferguson. Completed by K. F. Pantzer.* London: The Bibliographical Society.

Polverini Fosi, I. (1984) 'Crescenzi, Bartolomeo' in *DBI*, vol. 30.

Popplow, M. (1998) 'Protection and promotion: privileges for inventions and books of machines in the early modern period', *History of Technology* 20, 103–124.

Poulle, E. (1981) 'Fine, Oronce', in *DSB*, vol. 15 & 16.

Pyatt, E. (1983) *The National Physical Laboratory. A History.* Bristol: Adam Hilger Ltd.

Quaritch, B. (1887) *A General Catalogue of Books Offered to the Public at the Affixed Prices.* Vol. 1, *Manuscripts and Books Related to Them. Science. Periodical Literature. Romance of Chivalry.* London: G. Norman & Son.

Raven, J., H. Small, and N. Tadmor (eds) (1996) *The Practice and Representation of Reading in England.* Cambridge: Cambridge University Press.

Riccardi, P. [1870–1880] (1952) *Biblioteca matematica italiana: dalle origini della stampa ai primi anni del secolo XIX.* Milan: Görlich.

Rice, A. (1996) 'Augustus De Morgan: historian of science', *History of Science* 34, 201–240.

Richeson, A.W. (1966) *English Land Measuring to 1800: Instruments and Practices.* Cambridge, Mass.: Published jointly by the Society for the History of Technology and the MIT Press.

Rosen, E. (1981a) 'Schöner, Johannes', in *DSB*, vol. 11 & 12.

Rosen, E. (1981b) 'Regiomontanus, Johannes', in *DSB*, vol. 11 & 12.

Rossiter, M.W. (ed.) (1999) *Catching Up With the Vision. Essays on the Occasion of the 75th Anniversary of the Founding of the History of Science Society.* A Supplement to *Isis*, vol. 90.

Ruestow, E.G. (1973) *Physics at Seventeenth- and Eighteenth-Century Leiden: Philosophy and the New Science in the University.* The Hague: Martinus Nijhoff.

Russell, I. (1989) 'Purely by Coincidence: The Rangefinders of Barr and Stroud at the Battle of Jutland, 1916', in *Studies in the History of Scientific Instruments. Papers Presented at the 7th Symposium of the Scientific Instrument Commission of the Union Internationale d'Histoire et de Philosophie des Sciences, Paris 15–19 September 1987,* edited by C. Blondel, F. Parot, A. Turner, and M. Williams, 283–290. London: Rogers Turner Book.

Scarlett, S.M. (1978) *A Preliminary List of Catalogues and Advertising Literature Issued by the Cambridge Scientific Instrument Co. Ltd., the Cambridge and Paul Instrument Co. Ltd., and the Cambridge Instrument Co. Ltd.* Cambridge: Whipple Museum of the History of Science. Photocopied typescript.

Schaaf, W.L. (1981) 'Ozanam, Jacques', in *DSB*, vol. 9 & 10.

Schaffer, S. (1993) 'The Consuming Flame: Electrical Showmen and Tory Mystics in the World of Goods', in *Consumption and the World of Goods,* edited by J. Brewer, and R. Porter, 489–526. London: Routledge.

Searby, P. (1997) *A History of the University of Cambridge.* Vol. 3, *1750–1870.* Cambridge: Cambridge University Press.

Secord, J.A. (1985) 'Newton in the nursery: Tom Telescope and the philosophy of tops and balls, 1761–1838', *History of Science* 23, 127–151.

Shapin, S. (1992) 'Discipline and bounding: the history and sociology of science as seen through the externalism-internalism debate', *History of Science* 30, 333–369.

Sibum, O. (1995) 'Reworking the mechanical value of heat: instruments of precision and gestures of accuracy in early Victorian England', *Studies in History and Philosophy of Science* 26, 73–106.

Simcock, A.V. (1985) 'A Dodo in the Ark. The Genesis of the Museum of the History of Science in the Life of Robert T. Gunther', in *Robert T. Gunther and the Old Ashmolean,* edited by A.V. Simcock, 45–92. Oxford: Museum of the History of Science.

Simcock, A.V. (1994) 'Elucidatio Fabricae Ususque: Rambling Among the Beginnings of the Scientific Instrument Bookshelf', in *Learning, Language and Inventions. Essays Presented to Francis Maddison,* edited by W.D. Hackmann, and A. Turner, 273–296. Aldershot: Variorum; Paris: Société Internationale de l'Astrolabe.

Simmons, L., and J. Chidley (1982) 'H. Z. or the story of Heinrich Zeitlinger and the remarkable science catalogues at Sotheran', *Antiquarian Book Monthly Review* 9, 54–55.

Sorrenson, R. (1995) 'The State's Demand for Accurate Astronomical and Navigational Instruments in Eighteenth-Century Britain', in *The Consumption of Culture 1600–1800. Image, Object, Text,* edited by A. Bermingham, and J. Brewer, 263–271. London: Routledge.

Sotheran, H.C., and H. Zeitlinger (1921–1952) *Bibliotheca Chemico-Mathematica. Catalogue of Works in Many Tongues on Exact and Applied Science. Compiled and Annotated by H. Z. and H. C. S.* London: Henry Sotheran and Co.

Stafford, B.M. (1994) *Artful Science. Enlightenment Entertainment and the Eclipse of Visual Education.* Cambridge, Mass: The MIT Press.

Stewart, L. (1999) 'Other centres of calculation, or where the Royal Society did not count: commerce, coffee-houses and natural philosophy in early modern London', *BJHS* 32, 133–153.

Stroup, A. (1990) *A Company of Scientists. Botany, Patronage, and Community at the Seventeenth-Century Parisian Royal Academy of Sciences,* Berkeley & Los Angeles: University of California Press.

Symons, E.D.P. (1985) 'Two electrical book collections: the Ronalds and Thompson Libraries', *Institution of Electrical Engineering Proceedings* 132, 582–586.

Taton, R. (1981) 'Dalencé, Joachim', in *DSB*, vol. 3 & 4.

Taylor, E.G.R. (1954) *The Mathematical Practitioners of Tudor and Stuart England.* Cambridge: Cambridge University Press.

Taylor, E.G.R. (1966) *The Mathematical Practitioners of Hanoverian England 1714–1840.* Cambridge: Cambridge University Press.

Terraine, J. (1982) *White Heat. The New Warfare 1914–1918.* London: Sidgwick & Jackson.

Tesnière, V. (1993) 'Le livre de science en France au XIX siècle', *Romantisme* 80, 67–77.

Thackray, A. (1984) 'The Pre-History of an Academic Discipline. The Study of the History of Science in the United States, 1891–1941', in *Transformation and Tradition in the Sciences. Essays in Honor of I. Bernard Cohen,* edited by E. Mendelsohn, 395–420. Cambridge: Cambridge University Press.

Thompson, J.S, and H.G. Thompson (1920) *Silvanus Phillips Thompson. His Life and Letters.* London: T. Fisher Unwin.

Thoren, V.E. (1990) *The Lord of Uraniborg. A Biography of Tycho Brahe.* Cambridge: Cambridge University Press.

Topham, J. (1992) 'Science and popular education in the 1830s: the role of the *Bridgewater Treatises*', *BJHS* 25, 397–430.

Topham, J. (2000) 'A Textbook Revolution', in *Books and the Sciences in History,* edited by M. Frasca Spada, and N. Jardine, 317–337. Cambridge: Cambridge University Press.

Tribby, J. (1994) 'Club Medici: natural experiment and the imagineering of "Tuscany"', *Configurations* 2, 215–235.

Turner, A. (1973) 'Mathematical instruments and the education of gentlemen', *Annals of Science* 30, 51–88.

Turner, A. (1981) 'William Oughtred, Richard Delamain and the horizontal instrument in seventeenth-century England', *Annali dell'Istituto e Museo di Storia della Scienza* 6, 99–125.

Turner, A. (1987) *Early Scientific Instruments. Europe 1400–1800.* London: Sotheby's Publications.

Turner, A. (1989) 'Paper Print and Mathematics: Philippe Danfrie and the Making of Mathematical Instruments in late 16th century Paris', in *Studies in the History of Scientific Instruments. Papers Presented at the 7th Symposium of the Scientific Instrument Commision of the Union Internationale d'Histoire et de Philosophie des Sciences, Paris 15–19 September 1987,* edited by C. Blondel, F. Parot, A. Turner, and M. Williams, 22–42. London: Rogers Turner Book.

Turner, A. (1995) 'From mathematical practice to the history of science. The pattern of collecting scientific instruments', *Journal of the History of Collections* 7, 135–150.

Turner, A. (1998) 'Mathematical Instrument-Making in Early Modern Paris', in *Luxury Trades and Consumerism in Ancien Régime Paris. Studies in the History of the Skilled Workforce,* edited by R. Fox, and A. Turner, 63–96. Aldershot: Ashgate.

Turner, D.M. [1927] (1981) *History of Science Teaching in England*, New York: Arno Press.
Turner, G.L'E. (1980) *Essays on the History of the Microscope.* Oxford: Senecio Publishing Company.
Turner, G.L'E. (1989a) 'The origins of the Royal Microscopical Society', *Journal of Microscopy* 155, 235–248.
Turner, G.L'E. (1989b), '"Some curious old instruments". The assembly of the Royal Microscopical Society's collection of microscopes', *Journal of the History of Collections* 1, 149–166.
Van der Krogt, P. (1993) *Globi Neerlandici. The Production of Globes in the Low Countries.* Utrecht: HES Publishers.
Varley Jeffery, J. (1997), 'The Varley family: engineers and artists', *Notes and Records of the Royal Society of London* 51, 263–279.
Vogel, K. (1981) 'Köbel, Jacob', in *DSB*, vol. 7 & 8.
Wallis, P.J. (1968), 'William Oughtred's "Circles of Proportion" and "Trigonometries"', *Transactions of the Cambridge Bibliographical Society* IV, 372–82.
Wallis, P., and R. Wallis (1977) *Newton and Newtoniana 1672–1975. A Bibliography.* Cannon House Folkestone: Dawson.
Wallis, R.V., and P.J. Wallis (1993) *Index of British Mathematicians.* Part 3, *1701–1800,* Newcastle Upon Tyne: Project for Historical Biobibliography.
Walters, A.N. (1992) *Tools of Enlightenment: The Material Culture of Science in Eighteenth-Century England.* Ph.D. Thesis, University of California, Berkeley.
Walters, A.N. (1997) 'Conversation pieces: science and politeness in eighteenth-century England', *History of Science* 35, 121–154.
Warner, D.J. (1990) 'What is a scientific instrument, when it became one, and why?' *BJHS* 23, 83–93.
Warner, D.J. (1993) 'Introduction', in *Pike's Illustrated Catalogue of Scientific Instruments,* facsimile edition. San Francisco: Norman Publishing.
Warwick, A. (1994) 'The Worlds of Cambridge Physics', in *The Physics of Empire. Public Lectures,* edited by R. Staley, 57–86. Cambridge: Whipple Museum of the History of Science.
Waters, D.W. (1958) *The Art of Navigation in England in Elizabethan and Early Stuart Times.* London: Hollis and Carter.
Webster, R.S. (1981) 'Ramsden, Jesse', in *DSB*, vol. 11 & 12.
Weil, E. (1923) *Der Ulmer Holzschnitt im 15. Jahrhundert.* Berlin: Mauritius Verlag.
Weil, E. (1952) 'Milestones of Civilization', in *Talks on Book-Collecting Delivered Under the Authority of the Antiquarian Booksellers' Association,* edited by P. H. Muir. London: Cassell and Company.
Weil, H. (1995) 'Introduction', in *Catalogue of Books, Manuscripts, Photographs and Scientific Instruments Fully Described and Offered for Sale by Ernst Weil 1943–1965. Original Thirty-Three Catalogues Bound in Two Volumes,* edited by M. Martino. Glendale, CA: Jeff Weber.
Wells, E.B. (1983) 'Scientists' libraries: a handlist of printed sources', *Annals of Science* 40, 317–389.
Werskey, G. (1988) *The Visible College. A Collective Biography of British Scientists and Socialists of the 1930s.* London: Free Association Books.
Whipple, R.S. (1926) 'An old catalogue and what it tells us of the scientific instruments and curios collected by Queen Charlotte and King George III', *Proceedings of the Optical Convention,* Part 2, 502–528. London: Published by the Optical Convention.
Whipple, R.S. (1934) 'The evolution of the galvanometer. Report of a discourse given at the twenty-fourth Annual Exhibition of the Physical Society', *Journal of Scientific Instruments* 11, 37–43.
Whipple, R.S. (1942), 'Reminiscences of an instrument maker', *Journal of Scientific Instruments* 19, 178–183.
Whipple, R.S. (1951) 'John Yarwell or the story of a trade card', *Annals of Science* 7, 62–69.
Williams, M.E.W. (1994) *The Precision Makers. A History of the Instruments Industry in Britain and France, 1870–1939.* London: Routledge.
Willmoth, F. (1993) *Sir Jonas Moore: Practical Mathematics and Restoration Science.* Woodbridge: The Boydell Press.
Winkler, M.G., and A. van Helden (1993) 'Johannes Hevelius and the Visual Language of Astronomy', in *Renaissance and Revolution. Humanists, Scholars, Craftsmen and Natural Philosophers in Early Modern Europe,* edited by J.V. Field, and F.A.J.L. James, 97–116. Cambridge: Cambridge University Press.

Wood, P.B., and J.V. Golinski (1981) 'Library and archive resources in the history of science and medicine at the University of Leeds', *BJHS* 14, 263–281.
Wordsworth, C. [1877] (1968) *Scholae Academicae. Some Account of Studies at the English Universities in the Eighteenth Century.* London: Frank Cass & Co.
Zeitlin, J.I. (1971) 'Herbert M. Evans, 1882–1971', *Isis* 62, 507–509.
Zeitlinger, H. (1944) 'Newton's Library and Its Discovery' in *Library of Sir Isaac Newton. Presentation by the Pilgrim Trust to Trinity College Cambridge 30 October 1943*, 13–24. Cambridge: Cambridge University Press.
Zinner, E. (1941) *Geschichte und Bibliographie der astronomischen Literatur in Deutschland zur Zeit der Renaissance.* Leipzig: Verlag Karl W. Hiersemann.

Electronic resources: RLIN; English Short Title Catalogue.